The average person has no control over their money. Their employer dictates how much they earn. A bank or finance company dictates the type of home and car they can afford. Their credit card company dictates their amount of consumer spending. Of course, the average person has no money left over for giving or saving. Not only does the average person have no control over their money, their money has complete control over them.

In reading *On a Rock,* you will gain a new relationship with your money. You will no longer serve your money; your money will serve you. You will develop a solid foundation to build your finances. This foundation includes six components:

- your income
- your choices as a consumer
- your charitable giving
- your planned spending
- your intentional saving
- and your foundation held together with the mortar of your purpose.

On a Rock is an easy to read set of principles to help you create a solid financial foundation. These five components of your financial foundation directed by your purpose will give your money meaning and your life significance. Start reading it today to get your financial life in order.

23

On a Rock

Building Your Solid Financial Foundation

Lynn Schaal
Gus Brackett

Gus Brackett
Luke 9:13-17

Twelve Baskets Book Publishing, LLC

Twelve Baskets Book Publishing, LLC
48600 Cherry Creek Rd.
Rogerson ID 83302
www.12bookbaskets.com
gus@12bookbaskets.com

ISBN-13: 978-0-9841876-1-4
ISBN-10: 0-9841876-1-8

Printed in the U.S.A.

Contents

Prologue

How to Read This Book...

By opening this book, you have demonstrated an interest in changing your relationship with your money. Most people have problems with their finances, and too often, their money, or lack of money, dictates the course of their life. But by reading this book, you have a desire to change how your money works for you. Your money is simply a tool to make your life fulfilling. Using your money to create a purpose-filled life will not happen accidentally. It must be intentional and the work can be difficult, but the rewards are abundant.

On a Rock must be read actively. If this book is simply entertaining or amusing, you have missed the point. This book is a call to action to get your financial life in order. *On a Rock* explores the relationship you have with your money. With the concepts in this book, you can stop serving your money and make your money serve you.

In the next several pages, you will explore how to build a solid financial foundation. Your foundation is comprised of six basic components: Your Income (Chapter 2), Your Choices (Chapter 3), Your Giving (Chapter 4), Your Planned Spending (Chapters 5 and 6), Your Savings (Chapter 8), and all of this held together with the mortar of purpose (Chapters 7 and 9). To understand the relationship you have with money, Chapter 1 explores the concept of money and value.

On a Rock is best read with a pencil and paper to take notes and to actively walk through the steps prescribed. Underline passages that interest you and take note of concepts that you will explore further.

On a Rock was not designed to be placed on a shelf. When you finish, pass it on to someone else. Start with the people in your sphere of influence. Your spouse, your children, your friends, and your co-workers could all benefit from this book. After you learn these concepts, please be a blessing in the life of another by getting *On a Rock* in their hands as well.

1

YOUR MONEY

Traditions have perpetuated many myths about the Bible. For instance, in the Garden of Eden, God freely gave Adam and Eve everything, only commanding them to not eat from the Tree of Good and Evil. In almost every rendition of this story—book, movie, painting—this "forbidden fruit" is portrayed as an apple. The fact is, the Bible doesn't specify what kind of fruit Eve tasted. Every Christmas story includes the Magi, three wise men from the East who brought expensive gifts for Jesus and His family. However, the Bible says nothing about the number of Magi, just the number of gifts they bring. In fact, history suggests that only foolish men, not wise, would travel such great distances, and with such large treasures, without an extensive caravan. In addition, many jokes have the "pseudo-theological" notion that St. Peter meets everyone at the gates of heaven when they die. For that matter, the Bible does not state that when we die we enter heaven by first meeting anyone at the pearly gates, let alone all people going to heaven.

Since this book is about finances, perhaps the most notable Bible fallacy is the saying, "Money is the root of all evil." This assumption derives from the passage in 1 Timothy 6:10 that reads: *"For the love of money is the root of all kinds of evil."* (NKJV) As you can see, it is the *love* of money, or greed, that is the root of all evil, not money in and of itself. So why does money have such a bad reputation among both Christians and society in general?

First, let's take a look at what money actually is: its origination, its symbolic purpose, and a very brief account of its history. Perhaps the simplest explanation of money is currency. The $1, $5, $10, $20, and all of the coins are a physical representation of money, but this is an incomplete portrayal of the current monetary system. Money is a unit of exchange that represents a socially agreed upon value. But what does that really mean? Let me explain…

In the Beginning…of Money

Diverse cultures on different continents developed their monetary system at a distinct rate and timing. Some cultures, like the Egyptians, had an early monetary system around 3,000 BC while some secluded cultures still don't use money today. Primitive cultures used a barter system almost exclusively. A barter system is one where actual goods and services are exchanged for other goods and services. Farmer Dan has extra chickens but not enough grain, while Farmer Joe has plenty of grain but not enough chickens. So Dan and Joe swap chickens for grain.

This system works best without specialization. Specialization is when individuals focus their working efforts on creating one item of value instead of providing everything for themselves. A person who specializes must be able to trade his surplus for the other things he needs. For instance, if Seamstress Mary needs chickens, she must hope that Farmer Dan rips his shirt. Or if Dentist Robert needs grain, he must pray that Farmer Joe gets a toothache. With a barter system, it is difficult for specialized labor to develop. It is also difficult to accumulate wealth aside from the commodities you produce or barter.

To ease transactions, a primitive society would develop some form of scarce token to represent value in exchanges. This token was generally a commodity and took the form of almonds, butter, cattle, chocolate, coconuts, copper, feathers, dried fish, furs, gold, grain, salt, seashells, silver, tea, teeth, tobacco, and tusks to name just a few. As a result, this medium of exchange could open the door for specialization of labor. Transactions were standardized, and wealth could accumulate outside of goods produced. So now, Farmer Dan can pay Dentist Robert two gold coins for a tooth extraction, and Dentist Robert can exchange one gold coin with Farmer Joe for a measure of grain. Dentist Robert can save his other gold coin to purchase goods or services at a later date.

This system worked quite well, but there were some exceptions. As the number of tokens increased or decreased, the tokens became less valuable or more valuable respectively. As more gold was mined and minted into gold coins, the value of all coins decreased relative to the goods and services. In this situation, the gold coin that Dentist Robert used to purchase a measure of grain will only purchase half a measure of grain five years from now. The opposite can occur if there weren't enough tokens to transact business. Dentist Robert's gold coins will now buy two measures of grain five years from now. With the value of the currency fluctuating wildly, Dentist Robert would probably store his wealth in chickens instead of gold coins. Commodity tokens were—and still are for that matter—prone to consumption or spoilage and could cause this deflationary situation.

As civilization advanced and trade became less localized, the need for a more mobile form of currency developed. Banks would issue a paper note that represented an amount of gold. So instead of rolling out gold bars to purchase a home, a person could present the note to the seller, and the seller could either receive gold at the issuing bank or present it to another seller for goods or services.

In our country, the federal government nationalized this system in the early twentieth century, and the paper dollar was backed by gold. Through a series of political moves, the gold backing of the paper was eventually dropped. The United States government owns around 8,000 tons of gold housed in massive bunkers at Fort Knox, West Point, and other locations, but not a single ounce of this gold backs the US dollar. The gold supplies are simply part of the national treasure and are not part of the monetary system. The Federal Reserve Note, as the dollar is called, is no longer redeemable for gold. Because it can't be redeemed for gold, the phrase, "Payable to the Bearer on Demand," has been replaced by the more familiar, "In God We Trust." Without this gold backing, our entire monetary system of today is backed by decree of the government and society's trust in the system.

The Digitized Dollar

Today's system of money is even less tangible. Less than ten percent of the money supply is currency. The remainder is simply numbers on a digitized balance sheet in a bank or reserve. While we may carry cash, most of today's commerce is transacted with a credit card or some other electronic transfer system.

So what impact has this had on today's society? With the electronic money, the consumer mentality has flourished. As exchange becomes easier, we buy more things. You can purchase a pair of shoes from 500 miles away before you get dressed in the morning using a computer and a credit card. With that same credit card, you can purchase more goods and services in a month than you earn. Bills and membership payments are automatically withdrawn from your account to simplify your transactions. Goods or services that were once too expensive to purchase are easily purchased and paid off with interest over a series of months or years. With the inflation associated with paper money, money is less valuable over time, and this becomes a disincentive to saving.

In God We Trust

The monetary system is based strictly on trust and belief. While the government has decreed that dollars must be used to transact commerce, American society must consent to its use. If Americans loose trust in the viability of the dollar, they can barter or agree on another unit of exchange.

We trust that the government will maintain the value of the currency. We trust that sellers of goods and services will accept our dollars as an exchange. We trust that the dollars we receive for our labor is a true representation of the value we have created. This trust is so important that the government explains it as the full faith and credit of the U.S. government. Most writers about money explain the trust we have in money as faith. But there is a very stark difference between *trusting* in money and putting your *faith* in money. You can believe that money will have some type of value in this society. We can trust that the money we receive as wages can be used to purchase goods and services and can be used to store some measure of value for future use.

However, there is a real danger in putting faith in your money because you must understand the limitations of money. Many people will place their faith in inanimate or intangible money, and this is the problem with money. But money cannot feed your family, money cannot heal what ails you, and money cannot bring true peace into your life. The truth is, your hard work and God's provision can provide money to buy food to feed your family. While you can use your money to pay for medical services, all healing comes from God. And when you are in the midst of grave situations, no amount of money in your pocket can offer you the kind of peace your soul needs.

Money has no power other than as a unit of exchange. Money is not the root of all evil. Conversely, money itself is not a blessing. It is simply a unit of measure for wealth and exchange.

The Love of Money is the Root of All Evil

The conflict of greed and abundance is difficult for most Christians to sort out. Many believe that the accumulation of wealth is a manifestation of greed. This is not true. The Bible is dotted with Godly, wealthy individuals. Abraham, Isaac, and Jacob amassed great wealth in livestock, land, and servants. David, Solomon, and most of the kings lived opulent lifestyles. Throughout history, God has encouraged and enabled the accumulation of wealth. So how is this different from greed?

Greed has an aspect of idolatry that comes between man and God. Greed is manifest when someone places their accumulated wealth before God. Greedy people wrongly attribute their wealth to their own genius and gumption. They view their wealth as a replacement to God. They say: "God doesn't heal, money heals." Or, "God doesn't provide me with shelter, my money does." When money replaces God in a person's life, this is how greed is exhibited.

This conflict between wealth accumulation and greed is portrayed in Luke 18:18-25. A rich young man asks Jesus what he can do to have a closer relationship with God. Jesus, seeing the grip money has on this young man, tells him, *"Sell all that you have and distribute to the poor, and you will have treasure in heaven; and come, follow Me."* (NKJV) Jesus is not prohibiting the accumulation of wealth in this passage, but he is forcing the rich man to decide between his beloved riches and following Christ. Greed is personified in the rich man because he wrongly chooses his wealth instead of Christ. Given a similar situation, how would you respond? Again, this is not a prohibition of working hard, generating wealth, and saving; instead it is an issue of priority. Placing your money ahead of Christ is the "love of money" that Jesus warns us about.

The Magical Powers of Money

In today's society, money is given attributes that are wholly undeserved. The same false premise of, "Money is the root of all evil," is expressed in the phrase, "Money is the key to happiness," and both of these philosophies are flawed. There is a strong cultural desire to tie our emotions with our money. While this correlation is understandable, it is not accurate. Money is nothing more than a unit of measure. It is not a measure of our evil or our happiness. In that same rite, it is not a measure of our salvation or our condemnation. Many evil men in the Bible (Nimrod, Ahab) were wealthy beyond measure, while some of the Godliest men in the Bible (Job, Moses) lost their worldly possessions in following God.

Money is a unit of measure; nothing more and nothing less. A crucial first step in mastering our finances is to view money with this rationality. Money is not a status symbol. It is not security. It is simply a unit of measure.

On a Rock

A parable tells the story of two men; one wise and one foolish. The wise man builds his house on a rock and the foolish man builds this house on the sand. The wind and the storms predictably come. The house built on the rock withstands these outside forces and remains despite the storms. The house built on the sand faces the same wind and storms; but this house crumbles. The house with the solid foundation can weather the same wind and storms that destroy the house built on the sand.

This parable can be applied to several facets of life. When applied to your finances, the message is simple. Economic winds and storms will come. Is your financial foundation built on a rock or on the sand? In the next several chapters, you will learn what this "rock" is, as well as how to create this rock foundation upon which to build your finances. You will see how your work and labor is your most effective wealth-generating tool. You will learn the value of purposeful choice in making your consumer decisions. You will also learn the foundational aspects of giving, planning, and saving. Finally, you will learn to use your financial resources to fulfill your purpose.

2

YOUR INCOME

Almost everyone knows the Ten Commandments, and even people who can't list the Ten Commandments understand the concept. Children are taught these are the "big ones" *never* to be broken, and from which all of the law is derived. In addition, over the years, the commandments have been condensed into more manageable sound bytes. In one of the most memorable cinematic moments, Charlton Heston, as Moses, receives the Ten Commandments written on a rock wall by an animated pillar of fire. "Thou shalt have no other gods before me," the booming voice calls, as the rock is engraved. As the movie recalls the fourth commandment, the booming voice calls again, "Remember the Sabbath to keep it holy." Period. End of commandment.

This famous movie sound byte is great theater and may even be an effective means to learn the Ten Commandments. However, the Ten Commandments, especially the first four, are not easily condensed into sound bytes. I encourage you to read the commandments in their entirety (Exodus 20), but right now we will focus on this new sound byte: "Remember the Sabbath day, to keep it holy. Six days you shall labor and do all your work, but the seventh in the Sabbath of the Lord your

God." Notice the often forgotten portion: "Six days you shall labor and do all of your work." This commandment does not say, "Put in your time for forty hours and take Saturday and Sunday off." It doesn't say, "Work and labor as many hours as your employer allows." This commandment makes no exceptions for the unemployed or underemployed. This commandment implies and encourages creating your own work and being a self-starter. This statement of laboring six days and completing your work is quite clear.

The fourth commandment isn't simply about rest; it's about finding balance in your life. This commandment is about knowing when to work and when to rest and to commune with God. Many people complain they can't get ahead at work, or they can't keep up financially. They work forty hours every week and rest on Saturday and Sunday. However, God commands, not suggests, a greater commitment to work.

The Protestant Work Ethic in the Technological Age

The cultural norms of work have evolved and changed throughout history. In the era before Christ, Hebrew culture viewed work with contempt. It didn't start out that way; in Genesis 2:15, God commanded Adam to work and take care of the Garden of Eden. *"Then the LORD God took the man and put him in the garden of Eden to tend and keep it."* (NKJV) Adam was given the responsibility of caring for the entire earth and was promised great prosperity for this privilege. When sin entered the world, this ideal work situation was disrupted as described in Genesis 3:19. *"In the sweat of your face you shall eat bread; Till you return to the ground, For out of it you were taken; For dust you are, And to dust you shall return."*(NKJV) The notion of work was the same, but Adam's work was less productive, and now, work was viewed as punishment for sin. This historical view excluded the notion of fulfilling God's purpose in your labor; instead, work was a means to avoid starvation and poverty. This early Judaic tradition developed in spite of numerous Old Testament scriptures supporting the wisdom of work (Proverbs 10:14; Proverbs 13:4; Proverbs 20:13, Ecclesiastes 9:10).

At the height of the Greek and the Roman empires, they disdained work for secular reasons. In the millennium just before and just after Christ, work was considered vulgar, dishonoring, and undignified. Leisure was a status symbol that was a measure of a man's morality and wisdom. In both of these cultures, slaves were used extensively to accomplish all of the tasks beneath the sensibilities of the elite. A strong class system developed and work was only performed by the "lower classes." In these cultures, work was so disdained that they wouldn't even pay someone for their work.

During the Middle Ages, work still determined social status. But now, work was viewed as not only a means of sustaining life, but also a portal of creating wealth to share with those less fortunate. Different types of work were perceived as more or less Godly based on a hierarchy established by the elite. The work of the clergy and the ruling class was Godlier than physical labor and wages reflected this hierarchy. During this period, a person embarked on a particular line of work as a result of a calling of God. Work was now desirable, but was only considered fruitful based on the type of work.

During the 1600s, the Reformation brought about religious, political, and cultural shifts throughout Western Europe. Attitudes toward work changed during these turbulent times. As a leader in the Protestant movement, Martin Luther (1483-1586) taught that people could serve God through their work and that all work was spiritually equal. No job was superior from a spiritual perspective.

John Calvin (1509-1564), a French theologian, influenced Protestant views toward work more than any other. Calvin believed that all men, including the wealthy, must work to fulfill the will of God. Any wealth generated from their labors must be reinvested to finance greater profits. Work was no longer a curse, but a means of fulfilling God's calling. Your diligent work was now considered an outward expression of your commitment to Christ.

A prominent German economist named Max Weber (1864-1920) spent his career studying the connection between the Protestant Reformation and capitalism. He concluded that the Protestant Reformation directly changed economic structure based on these theological shifts. Weber coined the term "Protestant Ethic," which held that diligence, punctuality, deferred gratification, and hard work were attributes of Protestantism.

Today, technology has changed the way we view work. Technology has made us more productive, efficient and more connected. With cell phones, e-mail, the internet, and other connectivity tools, we can't get away from our work. With this technological revolution, attitudes toward work are again shifting. With a de-emphasis on the theological aspects of work, today's worker is motivated by fulfillment in their job. Employees work at their job for the intrinsic sense of accomplishment that the job provides. The non-Christian will view this fulfillment as a nebulous, difficult to quantify sense of satisfaction; but the Christian should view this sense of accomplishment as seeking, determining, and fulfilling God's purpose in your work life. This is the true essence of fulfillment.

Many people have several misconceptions about the role of work in their lives. Many hold a view like the Hebrews, Greeks, and Romans. Work is seen only as a means to avoid poverty and starvation. Others may view work like the Church of the Middle Ages. Work is only a means to generate wealth to give to the church and the impoverished. There is a hierarchy of jobs with the ministry as the highest form of work and menial labor as less than Godly.

Still others have a Reformation view of work. Work should be done for maximum profit, and this profit is an indication of your salvation. You should note, the Christian should seek an ever-increasing profit, but this is an indication of God's blessings, and not a reflection of your salvation.

Christians can also secularize their work in the technological revolution. Many of today's Christians live two separate lives: Their church life and their work life. They take a worldly approach to their work. Fulfillment is based on secular notions like recognition, advancement, achievement, and job satisfaction. In truth, Christians should find fulfillment in their work based on matching their talent and ability with God's purpose, and matching that purpose with their career. Christians mistakenly believe that the Lord's work is only done through the clergy. God's purpose is fulfilled through every line of work, the fruits of which are borne in a variety of ways.

Faith: the Currency of Heaven

Money is the currency of our world's economy…the Kingdom of Man. Here in the United States, a coin is only legal tender when the coin is intact.

Neither side of the coin can be defaced in any way. If one side should be defaced, the coin is then worthless. It has no monetary value; it is simply a piece of metal and cannot acquire any goods or services.

The Kingdom of God has an economy as well and a currency that is used in that economy. The currency of the Kingdom of God is called faith. The King of this Kingdom, God, has determined that faith will be the currency used to operate in the economy of His Kingdom. Everything in this Kingdom is acquired or appropriated by this currency. 2 Corinthians 5:7 says, *"the just shall live by faith."* (NKJV) Just as our money has two sides, faith, the currency of the Kingdom of God, also has two sides. One side of the coin of faith is "belief;" the other side of the coin is "action." Both sides must be intact to be spent in the Kingdom of God. If one side or the other is defaced, then faith does not exist, and if faith does not exist, nothing can be acquired.

Belief is a great thing. All people of all societies believe various things. However, in the economy of the Kingdom of God, belief by itself is not enough to operate within this economy. Specifically, this belief must be based upon truth, and truth that is found in God's word becomes the source of belief for the Christian. Action is great as well. All people of all societies do various things. However, in the economy of the Kingdom of God, action by itself will not operate within this economy. *Any* action does not meet the requirements; it is action tied directly to belief about the truth of God's word. When belief and action are united, faith is generated.

This is crucial to the life of any Christian and answers why many Christians cannot acquire things from the Kingdom of God. Many believe that God *can*. They believe that He could do anything if He wanted, and they contend that belief alone will bring about the promises of God. Likewise, many Christians *do* good things, and they contend that action alone will bring about the promises of God. Sadly, this leads many Christians to the mindset that based upon either what they believe or how they act, they can acquire things from the Kingdom of God. But only through faith as a combination of belief and action can things like wisdom, protection, healing, peace, and provision be acquired from the Kingdom of God; faith is always comprised of belief and action.

Jesus the Carpenter, Paul the Tentmaker, Peter the Fisherman

Jesus spent most of his natural life as a carpenter. As a young boy, he learned his trade from Joseph, his father. He learned the intricacies of wood finishing and spent years developing his skills and abilities as a carpenter. Jesus worked hard to develop and practice his craft.

The apostle Paul was perhaps the greatest missionary for the Christian faith. Paul was also a tentmaker. His father taught him this trade and Paul practiced tent making throughout his life, and was skillful enough to generate income. Paul never asked the small churches that he planted to fund his ministry. Whenever he needed money, he self-sufficiently plied his trade.

The apostle Peter preached some of the most poignant sermons after Christ's death. Peter was also a fisherman. He learned and developed sailing skills, and he was skilled at casting and drawing a net. Whenever Peter was distressed or just needed an escape, he would pursue his passion: fishing. Jesus, Paul, and Peter all developed a trade. They all learned, practiced, and worked at their wealth-generating trade.

You may not be a carpenter, a tentmaker, or a fisherman, but the principles of developing a trade are the same. Learn your trade, and then diligently perfect your trade through practice, and increase your knowledge through learning.

First, learn your trade. Jesus never went to college, so do you need to go? It depends on your talent and ability, and ultimately the career field you choose. Higher Education is a prerequisite for many professional occupations. For many other jobs, the ability to learn is more important than the knowledge learned. This ability can be developed at college. On the other hand, many careers can be learned at trade school or community college. Many people use college to postpone working for four years. The basics of many jobs can be learned in a short amount of time. Also, apprenticeships and on-the-job training are available. Learning while getting paid is an appealing option for many. With an apprenticeship or on-the-job training, the training is only as good as your willingness to learn. Opportunities abound for someone learning a trade.

Developing a trade is where many people fail in the marketplace. If you don't perfect your trade and continue learning, your job will become static and eventually outdated, regardless of the industry.

Continuing formal education is certainly one way to develop your skills. If you are just stockpiling degrees and certifications to boost your resume, then eventually an employer will want proof that you have the knowledge and skills behind all of those pieces of paper. Just remember that formal education is only one of many ways to advance your career.

Then, you should live a lifestyle of developing your skills. You should read trade publications and attend trade conventions and seminars. Take advantage of any voluntary training programs and use mandatory training as a means to develop. Understand how your company earns profits and how your position contributes to that profit. Learn the basics of other positions in your company. Ask your employer questions. Most employers are passionate about their company and enjoying sharing what they know. Ask them about the work itself, but also ask them the best way to develop skills for your trade.

You may have heard the axiom, "If you do what you are passionate about, you will never work a day in your life." There is a great deal of truth in that statement. Marrying your natural giftings with your passion will help you realize this axiom. Our Creator placed within each person a natural skill-set. We could call them "gifts" as well. The Apostle Paul wrote to the Roman church about this in Romans 12:6-8:

> *God has given each of us the ability to do certain things well. So if God has given you the ability to prophesy, speak out when you have faith that God is speaking through you. If your gift is that of serving others, serve them well. If you are a teacher, do a good job of teaching. If your gift is to encourage others, do it! If you have money, share it generously. If God has given you leadership ability, take the responsibility seriously. And if you have a gift for showing kindness to others, do it gladly.* (NLT)

People are all gifted in a variety of ways, but one thing is true: all people have unique gifts that can bring about personal satisfaction and help society at large. If you are unsure of your personal giftings, there are assessments with which you can concretely discover them. Marry your giftings with what you are truly passionate about, and you too can be motivated by a career that is more about purpose that just making a buck.

How to be a Good Employee

You are the owner of a small business with two employees. Both employees are very similar. They are very competent, have similar skill levels and are dedicated workers when they are on the job. But both employees have a problem.

Employee number one has a drinking problem. He drinks heavily every weekend, but has never been intoxicated on the job. On Monday night he is part of a bowling league where he drinks heavily. Every Thursday night he starts the weekend early with several drinks at the bar. Every Tuesday and Friday, this employee is forty-five minutes late for work. Early in the afternoon, he becomes tired, irritable and his productivity suffers. The rest of the week, he is a model employee.

Employee number two is a Christian. He volunteers at his church every weekend and attends every service, but never proselytizes on the job. On Sunday night he attends church and fellowships with members of the church until late in the night. Every Wednesday night he attends Wednesday service and stays late playing basketball with some of the kids. Every Monday and Thursday morning this employee is forty-five minutes late for work. Early in the afternoon, he becomes tired, irritable, and his productivity suffers.

In your mind, as an employer, you have two identical employees. From a positive perspective, they are skilled and competent. They are also both forty-five minutes late two days a week. An employer doesn't see the off-the-job motive; he will just see two employees who, for whatever reason, can't show up on time. If the employer is not a Christian, he may add a level to his outlook. He may think, the drunk is always late, so I don't want to be a drunk; and the Christian is always late, so I don't want to be a Christian, either.

This is the challenge of finding balance as a Christian. Worship and fellowship are important, but you also have responsibilities at work. Part of your responsibility is as an ambassador for Christ to the world. Being Christian is not a valid excuse from work.

What specifically is an employer looking for in an employee? To understand the answer, you must first understand the role of the employee. Some people think that the purpose of a job is just making money. They put in their time, and the employer will give them a salary and benefits. The employer views this transaction differently.

The employer hires employees to increase the productivity of his business and to earn profit. An employee is valuable to an employer only if they create more value for the employer than the employer pays in salary, benefits, taxes, training, and the internal costs associated with maintaining your employment. If you don't create more value for your employer than they pay you, then the employer will terminate either you or your position. Think of this next time you complain, "I make my boss a lot more money than he pays me." Without this profit, your employer will not stay in business or maintain your job.

Creating value for your employer is the foundation of the ethic of transactional employment. In a transactional setting, your employer will set the terms of employment. He will specify your responsibilities and will have an expectation that you fulfill your tasks. These responsibilities in a completely transactional relationship will be fully spelled out. He will tell you exactly what he wants accomplished and the time you will spend accomplishing it. In exchange for your labor and work, your employer will pay you a predetermined salary and benefits. The transaction is simple; you perform the work like he wants and your employer will pay you.

For a Christian, understanding this basic ethic is crucial. This aspect of work must be understood because being paid what you didn't earn is the same as stealing. Many people in larger companies make a career of this activity, but with an astute manager, the consequence will be termination or layoff.

While understanding and applying this basic ethic is important, Christians are held to an even higher standard. Jesus speaks of servanthood in Luke 17:7-10 by describing the essence of servanthood:

> *And which of you, having a servant plowing or tending sheep, will say to him when he has come in from the field, "Come at once and sit down to eat?" But will he not rather say to him, "Prepare something for my supper, and gird yourself and serve me till I have eaten and drunk, and afterward you will eat and drink?" Does he thank that servant because he did the things that were commanded him? I think not. So likewise you, when you have done all those things which you are commanded, say, "We are unprofitable servants. We have done what was our duty to do."* (NKJV)

A servant has been in the field all day plowing or tending sheep. When the servant returns from the field, instead of cleaning, dining, and relaxing, the servant prepares his master's dinner and serves the master until he is finished. Only then can the servant eat and drink. The servant performs all of this without a "thank you." The servant does this because it is his duty.

From an employer/employee perspective, this story is about understanding roles of each party. A servant, or employee, has the moral obligation to perform the duties for which they were hired. In our day and age, employees must know that by accepting a paycheck, they are morally committed to honor their end of the agreement.

A Servant's Heart

A Christian should have a servant's heart. This applies to employees, employers, the unemployed, and to everyone. From an employee perspective, simply maintaining a transactional relationship is not good enough. The Christian is not just to work for money. As a servant, he must place his employer's best interest ahead of his own. If an employer has this same attitude, not to his employees, but to their clients, then the business will prosper. In fact, some professions by law must adopt this way of doing business. Lawyers, accountants, and other professionals have a fiduciary responsibility to their clients. They must put the self-interest of their client above their own self-interest. They not only work for the person who hires them, but they must also serve their needs and desires.

Every Christian employee has this type of responsibility to their employer. Understand that having a servant's heart in the workplace is not burdensome. Every Christian should have a desire to serve Christ. This service is most easily fulfilled by serving man.

"Bondservants, obey in all things your masters according to the flesh, not with eyeservice, as men-pleasers, but in sincerity of heart, fearing God. And whatever you do, do it heartily, as to the Lord and not to men, knowing that from the Lord you will receive the reward of the inheritance; for you serve the Lord Christ." (Colossians 3:22-24, NKJV) This scripture has great wisdom for the Christian employee. Whatever we do, on the job or off the job, do it as unto the Lord. The Christian that separates his spiritual life from his secular life may think this servanthood merely involves volunteering for "church work" or charity work. While this work is important and should be done, we also serve our fellow man while on the job. Getting paid doesn't exempt you from servanthood.

Part of being a servant is doing your job with a joyful heart. Providing food for someone, building their home, making them well are all ways to serve. Providing an entertaining distraction or making someone more productive are excellent ways to serve. Protecting or defending someone's life or property can be your capacity of servanthood. Virtually every job can be and should be viewed through the prism of servanthood.

With this approach, you must remember that your boss can guide and direct your actions. You ultimately must serve his clientele his way. You may have very little discretion in operations, but you have complete control over your attitude.

This notion of fiduciary responsibility and servanthood should not be burdensome financially to you. On the contrary, it should make you a more valuable employee. Someone with a servant's heart who places the company's agenda before their own will advance in their career. While a transactional employee quibbles and fumes over how little a raise they got and how their benefits are inadequate, your employer will see you as someone who is a dependable, diligent, and committed worker. When economic times get tough, and jobs are cut, a company will retain as many profitable employees as they can.

With a servant's heart, remember that you have other responsibilities. Your loyalties should lie with your employer only as the marketplace dictates. If a better job comes up, you should not be constrained by servanthood to remain at your position. Servanthood does not mean you are stuck at your job. If your talents and abilities will be appreciated financially somewhere else, you should consider a change. If your servanthood is taken for granted, don't change your attitude as so many do; change your job.

A final caution on servanthood: when Daniel was asked to defy his God by praying to the Persian ruler, Daniel refused and was famously thrown in the lion's den. God rewarded his faithfulness by sparing him and promoting him. A servant will do what is in the best interest of their employer. If a misguided employer asks you to do something immoral, unethical, illegal, or against your Christian values, you should refuse. Not only should you refuse, but you should find a more appropriate employer and report illegality to the proper authorities. Servanthood does not mean compromising your values.

A valuable employee displays several traits. Employees expressing these traits consistently are more valuable to an employer. A servant's attitude is the first trait from which all of the others are derived.

Punctuality

Different societies have different views on time. Some cultures have a more relaxed view of time, and in these, if you begin at nine o'clock, it really means 9:15

or 9:30. As an American, you do not live in a society where this is acceptable. American culture insists on punctuality.

Being late is rude and can really add up over time. The employee who shows up ten minutes late for work every day for a year is essentially stealing five work days per year from their employer (50 weeks, 5 day week, 8 hour day). If you make $100 per day, you will be stealing $500 per year from you employer. If you steal money and not time, it is called embezzlement. Stealing time is not forgotten by an employer.

This fact focuses on the transactional nature of employment. The Christian is held to a higher standard. Your duty is to work during the time your employer expects. Your employer will not notice if you are there; that is your duty. But he *will* notice if you are absent. If you were an employer promoting from within, and the choice for promotion is between two equally qualified individuals, which of these would you chose: the employee who is always on time and finishes his work after closing time, or the other employee who shows up late periodically only to wrap up his work early, bide his time for the last fifteen minutes, and then bolt out the door as the whistle is blowing. Which employee would you promote? Which one would you lay off?

Punctuality is an outward expression of your servant's heart. If you genuinely want your job, and to serve your fellow man, then you will be on time, or better yet, a little bit early. Being on time for work shows everyone, including your boss, that you care about your job.

Clean and appropriately attired

Long gone are the power suit and the power tie. Some professionals today have never worn a tie. "Casual Fridays" are evolving into "casual as often as we can get away with it." Being clean and appropriately dressed is a serious social issue. In the workplace, your outward appearance speaks volumes to your employer and your company's customers. Your attire is the baseline from which your degree of professionalism is judged.

In today's workplace, determining appropriate attire is increasingly difficult. The janitor at many internet companies is dressed classier than the CEO. The teller at the bank wears fine business attire and the president of the bank wears golf slacks and a golf shirt. What image should an employee present through their dress?

If your company has a uniform or a dress code, follow the code. Policies like these remove all ambiguity. With a uniform, your company has spent thousands if not millions of dollars for their employees to present a consistent image. You are an individual, and you should let your individuality shine through; but be an individual on your own time. Wear your uniform, and wear it as your employer specifies.

With a dress code, follow the letter and the spirit of the code. Dress codes were not designed so that employees could get as close to breaking the code as possible without getting reprimanded. If your dress code calls for a tie, wear a nice one and not a cartoon character tie in protest. Understand the image your company portrays and conform to this image.

If your company has no policy, then follow the lead of your supervisor on what is appropriate. If you work on a construction crew, then a three piece suit is not appropriate. However, you don't need to be the guy who works without his shirt. Your boss wears his work shirt; and so should you. If you work at a professional office where blue jeans and T-shirts are appropriate, then make sure you don't have holes in your pants and wear only your best T-shirts. If your boss wears a blazer but no tie, then a blazer and no tie is appropriate. If your boss wears a three piece suit, then you will need at least a suit and tie. If your direct supervisor is a slob, then you may want to take your lead from his supervisor. Once you become the boss or start your own business, then you can decide what is professional. Until then, you must adapt to the culture or tone set by the employer.

Competent

Competence in the workplace involves two critical components. First, you must know your job and continually learn to be more efficient. Second, you must organize and manage yourself to accomplish your tasks. We have already discussed the importance of education to develop your job skills. To amplify this point, learning does not occur only at a school. However, outside of school, you must take the initiative to find educational opportunities. This can be books, trade magazines and papers, seminars, conventions, and just asking questions of your boss and co-workers.

Managing your self is an important aspect of competence. You should keep your workspace sufficiently crganized so you can efficiently operate your tool. Whether your tool is a shovel or a computer, organizing your workspace is a critical component of competency.

Next, you must organize your thought. Unless you have a photographic memory, you must record your duties and instructions. PDA's are an excellent tool for this if you can operate them effectively, but for most employees, a pen and a pad of paper to jot down notes is sufficient. The paper can be big enough to fit on your desk or small enough to fit in your pocket. Suppose your boss gives you a list of six things to accomplish in a day. If you complete five tasks extraordinarily well, but forget the sixth, then your boss will notice the sixth, uncompleted task. This simple means for remembering tasks is also an excellent place to write down profit creating ideas you may have for your boss. Your ingenious ideas are only as good as you ability to remember them.

Competency includes all of the skills necessary to do your job effectively. Learning and perfecting your skills is not enough. You must employ those skills in such a way to create value and profit for your employer. What good are your skills to your employer if you can't effectively perform tasks?

Self-starter

An employee with a servant's heart is a self-starter. With transactional employment, your boss must tell you to do everything. As a self-starter, there are tasks you can complete without instruction. If there is something amiss in your work area, a self-starter will fix it or clean it up without the boss telling them. If your boss gives you the same instruction every day, a transactional employee will wait for that instruction every day; a self-starter will perform the repetitive task without prompting. A self-starter will seek out more work if all his duties are completed while a transactional employee will take advantage of this down time to loaf.

A self-starter will seek out ways to increase their company's bottom line. A self-starter will discern fundamentally how the company operates. At a minimum, the self-starter will help keep the organization functioning. A self-starter will also find ways to make the business more profitable. While a transactional employee dwells on making his job easier, the self-starter thinks about the profitability of the company

\- -

Your work is the greatest wealth generating tool that you have. As such, you should take your work seriously. You should develop a servant's attitude toward your work. People who work solely for money don't make very much. People who develop a servant's heart are more valuable in the marketplace and subsequently earn a greater income. Your skills and abilities are developed through life long education. You must be punctual, clean, competent, and a self starter. Finally, hard work is rewarded in this society.

Many people underestimate the importance of their work in building their financial foundation. With a limited income, it becomes difficult to balance your spending with your earning. Without an income, it becomes impossible. Your work, though, can be and should be so much more.

Your work is the source from which many of the blessings in your life flow. Your work will provide for yourself and your family. Your work is the source of money that can be the beginning of blessings in other people's lives. With a servant's heart, your work is a means for serving and, in that way, a blessing to others through your actions. If you understand this, your work can be a blessing to you, your family, your community, and the greater society in which you interact. God is waiting to bless those who accept His blessings through hard work.

On a Rock: Your Income

Your financial foundation begins with your income. The amount of money you earn determines how the remaining foundation will be configured. Many people accept the level of income they have, but so much more can be achieved by someone who develops a servant's heart and creates value for others.

This chapter contains specific directives on how to strengthen your income. First, you must learn, practice, and develop a trade. Next, you will create the most value for your employer and for yourself by developing a servant's heart. Finally, your income can be the cornerstone of your financial foundation if you fulfill your purpose through your work. To become a valuable employee with a servant's heart, you must develop the following traits: punctuality, clean and appropriate attire, competence, and being self-starter.

Your income is the first building block of your solid financial foundation. The remaining building blocks of choice, giving, planned spending, and savings all rely on a steady and robust income.

Your solid financial foundation:

- Income

3

YOUR CHOICES

There is a parable that tells of a man who travels to a far away country, and in order to tend to his affairs while he is gone, the man distributes his wealth in talents of gold to three of his servants. The first servant is given five talents of gold, the second is given two talents of gold, and the third is given one talent of gold. The man who was given five talents of gold invested the gold in trade and earned another five talents. Similarly, the second servant traded his gold to earn two more talents. The third servant dug a hole and buried his talent of gold in the ground.

When the master returned, he took account of his servants' activities and asked each one how they had used the money. The first servant reported he had taken the five talents and turned them into five more talents. The master praised this servant by saying, "Well done good and faithful servant; you were faithful over a few things, so I will make you ruler over many things."

Upon inspection, the second servant declared he had taken the two talents of gold and doubled it to four talents. Again, the master praised his servant by saying, "Well done good and faithful servant; you have been faithful over a few things, so I will make you ruler over many things."

Finally, the master questioned the third servant concerning the one talent he received. This servant answered by saying, "I was afraid, so I went and hid your talent in the ground. Look, there you have what is yours." And the servant handed the master back the one talent he had been given. To this man, the master gave a much different reply, "You wicked and lazy servant. You ought to have deposited my money with the bankers, and at my coming I would have received back my own with interest." The master then ordered another servant, "Take the talent from him and give it to him who has ten talents."

This parable is summarized in Matthew 25:29: *"For to everyone who has, more will be given, and he will have abundance; but from he who does not have, even what he has will be taken away."*(NKJV)

This parable is even more insightful when you place it in a context of today. At the time this story was spoken, a talent of gold was roughly worth one year's salary to a laborer. Today, an average salary in the United States is slightly more than $50,000, so if this allegory was told today, the figures for the three servants would be: $250,000 for the first, $100,000 for the second, and $50,000 for the third.

The doubling of an investment is also very practical. To double their money in ten years, they would need a return of 7.2%. If they invested in a more risky, but growing small business that returned 20%, the investment would double in four years.

The focus should be with the third servant. Given a year's wage, what did he do with it? He just buried it in the ground. He wasn't even smart enough to save a portion of it in the bank.

Today, people don't bury money in the ground. They don't even hide money beneath their mattresses. In burying a talent of gold, the third servant knew that the gold would retain its value, but it would not grow. A similar act would be using your money to buy items that may retain their value, but will not increase in value. The modern equivalent of burying money in the dirt would be spending all of it on "stuff." A collection of big screen TV's, video games, designer clothing, and cars you can't afford, a house that is too big, and toys for both young and old are modern versions of burying a talent of gold in the dirt. So what type of servant are you? Do you invest your year's wage with the intent of doubling your wealth? Do you at least put a portion of your year's wage in a bank to draw interest? Or, are you like the third servant, burying your year's wage in a variety of retail stores?

"But look," you may tell your master, "I have the newest HDTV. I have the latest sports car to show for my years of labor. I have thousands of dollars of trinkets, gadgets, and electronics to show for your talent of gold."

Would your master respond, "Well done good and faithful servant?" Or would you hear, "You wicked and lazy servant?"

Choices

Fundamentally, personal finance is about choice. However, many people view their financial lives from the perspective of circumstance. "I lost my job and ended up in bankruptcy." Or, "I'm stuck in a dead-end career." Or, "I found myself in $15,000 of credit card debt." The truth is, life is not a series of circumstances; it is a series of choices. And so it is in the realm of finances. Understanding the short and long term consequences of your choices is foundational in managing your wealth.

Choices are typically based on a set of priorities. People prioritize their lives differently. Some prioritize based on emotion and whim, while others set their priorities based on convenience or greed. A person spending his rent money at the bar has prioritized his pleasure over shelter. The family that spends $10,000 per year on the holidays, but has nothing saved for their children's education has prioritized an event today over future needs. The most effective means for setting priorities in your life is with prayer, thought, and by writing your priorities down. Writing down your priorities forces you to consider your priorities rationally instead of emotionally. In Chapters 5 and 6, you will create a prioritized spending list as part of a spending plan.

We have very little control over some events and needs we face in life. We have no control over a medical emergency, rising prices, or job layoff. But, we have complete control over a major portion of our lives, and many of the circumstances we find ourselves in are a result of choices we made previously. We can also plan for the emergencies that we have very little control over. In order to better understand the reasons behind the choices we make, let's explore the difference between needs and wants.

Needs

Basic human needs include food, clothing, and shelter. If these needs are not met, your health and life will be threatened. In the United States, it is rare for someone to not have these needs met, as even most people living below the poverty line have these three basic needs, albeit sometimes with assistance. Ours is a country where obesity is more of a problem than starvation, where people spend more on a change of clothes than a worker in a third world country makes in a year, and where people own two, three or more houses. In a country like ours, it is often taken for granted that these basic needs will be easily met. How we meet these basic needs will determine what we can do with the balance of our spending.

Most people add other bona fide needs to their spending. In a mobile society, transportation becomes a need. Unless you live in an apartment above your work, or next to a grocery and department store, then you will need transportation. Whether you need access to public transportation, a bicycle, a simple car, or a Ferrari, getting around is typically a need.

Health care and health insurance should be viewed as a need. We are blessed with perhaps the best health care system in the world, as doctors, nurses, medicines, and the vaccines of today are so competent, many deadly diseases or ailments are no longer lethal. The system is good, but not free. The health care crisis in America is less of a health crisis, and more of a financial crisis. Most personal bankruptcies are a result of catastrophic health care costs. We should position our financial life to take advantage of this health care system.

Keeping the power on may also be viewed as a need. What good is shelter without heat? How effective is your food without the means to prepare it? Paying your utilities should also be considered a need.

The money we have remaining once our basic needs are met is called disposable income. As we make consumer choices about our needs, remember one principle. The greater your disposable income, the more resistant you are to financial crisis. If you are barely able to make your house and car payment, pay utilities, insure your property and family, and buy groceries, then any reduction in your income will seriously strain your finances.

The way we meet our needs will determine what other spending we can do. Everyone could live at a basal level, spending very little money to meet their needs. Living in this era affords us an abundant life where we meet our needs well beyond this basal level. This abundance should be celebrated and embraced. However, this abundance mentality should not lead to excess and living beyond our ability to generate income.

Wants

The hallmark of a free market economy is choice. We aren't limited to just basic transportation. We can choose a car over public transportation. We can choose a passenger car over an SUV. We can choose domestic over foreign. We can choose from innumerable models from three different car companies. We even get to choose the color we want. At the grocery store, we can choose from four different types of milk from three different brands. Entire aisles are devoted to snack food or beverage choices. And the choices become even more daunting for our entertainment dollar. We are entertained by toys, recreation, television, movies, music, books, periodical, live performances, the internet, and all of these in numerous genres and countless delivery methods.

In this economic climate, businesses will spend thousands, millions, and billions on marketing so you will spend money on their product. In a crowded marketplace, they must convince you that their product is the greatest value, either the lowest cost, or the best product. As marketers have advanced their trade, they are positioning many wants as something you need. They are also positioning many needs so that you will spend more money to fill your needs. Most of your peers don't notice or care about the products you buy, but marketers want you to think that your peers really do care.

Most wants, like needs, are obvious. All form of entertainment should be viewed as wants. We have heard the adult say they couldn't live without cable television, or the younger person say they will die if they can't go to a certain concert. Obviously, we know they are being overly dramatic when making such statements. While cable TV or social events aren't necessary for life, many people are defined by their entertainment and hobbies.

Wants can also include travel, leisure, recreation, and general pampering. Wants typically make life more enjoyable. These wants will help us relax and refresh from the stresses of life. Wants are not bad, but like everywhere else you spend money, you are constrained by the amount of money you make. If you had limitless wealth, your wants would still be constrained by your finite time to enjoy them. You should also discern whether your wants are fulfilling something in your life. Exercise is noble and necessary, but millions of unused pieces of exercise equipment litter American homes. The same applies to unused memberships and subscriptions. Like every other consumer choice, wants should be evaluated prayerfully, thoughtfully, and with a pen and paper to determine if it is affordable.

Some wants are only a measure of status. With these purchases, a consumer is trying to engender some type of ego-based envy among their peers. Whether you strive for respect, glamour, perceived wealth, or just friendship, you will find status purchases quite empty. Most of your peers don't care what you buy, and if they do, you probably should reevaluate your friendship.

Wants purchased on the basis of status will be unfulfilling and will most likely drain your wealth. Likewise, when your needs are met based on status, or a need to impress, this typically leads to financial instability. If you own a house you can't afford, a car whose payments are as much as a house payment, clothes that are the newest, most expensive fashions, and you dine out nightly at expensive restaurants, then you are seeking status through your needs. You will come to find this type of life very temporal and wholly unsatisfying. Remember the principle, the greater your disposable income, the more resistant you are to financial crisis. People who spend for status will employ too much of their income on needs and will have very little cushion left for an economic storm.

We Make a Lot, But We Spend a Lot Too

Many professional athletes make exorbitant salaries. A few years back, one of the player's unions went on strike to secure higher salaries for the players. A reporter asked a superstar to justify the salary increase because he already made a lot of money. The player replied, "Yeah, we make a lot, but we spend a lot too." This statement sounds very empty to someone with a more limited income, but the principle should be explored. Most people can satisfy their basic needs, but they spend as much or more than they earn. To remedy this situation, they must either earn more or spend less. Here's a real life example:

A financial planner consults with a client. The client is a podiatrist with a thriving practice, but he can't seem to make ends meet. He wants help from the planner to budget his affairs.

"Let's start by filling out an income statement," the planner says. "How much to you make after taxes?"

"Oh, let me see. I clear about $120,000 a year after taxes," the doctor replies.

"Ten thousand a month," the planner exclaims. "How could you possibly have trouble balancing your budget?"

"I don't know. That's why I came to you."

"Okay, Okay. How much do you spend on your mortgage each month?"

"I spend $4,000 each month on my house."

"No, no. Just the payment," the planner says. "We don't need utilities, property taxes, and maintenance yet."

"Well," the doctor says as he looks down at his hands, "that *is* my payment. It's a really nice house, and, you know, I am a doctor; people expect me to live in a big house."

"How much do you spend on your car?"

"About $1,500 a month."

"Good grief," the planner says. "Let me guess, as a doctor, people expect you to buy a really nice car."

"It's actually a lease. Well, *two* leases: one for my sports car and one for my wife's SUV," the doctor smiles as he replies.

"How about clothing? How much do you spend?"

"Let me see. We typically spend $1,100."

"Is that per month?"

"Yeah, that's per month."

"For how many people?"

"That is me, my wife and my son."

This conversation continues until the income statement is filled out and the planner hands the following figures to the doctor.

Monthly Income Statement

Income		
	Salary	*$10,000*
Expenses		
	Housing	*$4,000*
	Transportation	*$1,500*
	Utilities	*$1,000*
	Clothing	*$1,100*
	Food	*$800*
	Medical	*$200*
	Entertainment	*$1,400*
	Charitable giving	*-0-*
	Total	*$10,000*

The financial planner sighs. "Every month you earn $10,000, but at the end of that month you have very little to show for your efforts. You have no savings, no retirement, and no money saved for your son's education. Let me teach you a lesson in perspective."

The planner opens his desk drawer and pulls out a yellow sheet of paper. The name was crossed out but all of the numbers were there.

"Take a look at this budget I helped a refugee from Central Asia prepare. When he got here, he had nothing but a willingness to work and a desire to learn."

The planner hands the paper to the doctor. The doctor studies the figures.

Monthly Income Statement		
Income		
	Salary	*$1,000*
Expenses		
	Rent	*$300*
	Transportation	*-0-*
	Utilities	*-0-*
	Clothing	*$50*
	Food	*$350*
	Medical	*-0-*
	Entertainment	*-0-*
	Charitable giving	*$100*
	Total	*$800*

"You can't live like this!" the doctor says.

"*You* couldn't, but he does," the planner replies. "He and his family of five live in a small apartment. They walk everywhere they go and sometimes it is great distances. They shop at thrift stores, give ten percent of everything they make to their church and still save $200 every month. That's why he talked to me. He wanted to know how to preserve his new found wealth."

The doctor shakes his head with his eyes still fixed on the paper. "So what you're saying," the doctor says, "is I need to watch my spending."

"As we can see, it's not what you earn that makes you wealthy. It's what you spend and save. Like most people, you don't need to cut very much spending to get your budget under control."

This maxim is the foundation of consumer choice: "It's not what you earn that makes you wealthy; it is how you spend and save." Your income is limited and your spending should reflect this. Most people could live fulfilling and financially secure lives just by cutting out the junk.

A Christian Perspective on Need and Wants

Many Christians have a mental quandary understanding where our "needs" and "wants" fit into the fabric of our lives. There are two ways of thinking regarding needs and wants. One way of thinking says that God only will provide for our needs. The scripture that supports this ideology is in the Apostle Paul's letter to the Philippians, *"And my God shall supply all your* ***need*** *according to His riches in glory by Christ Jesus."* (Philippians 4:19, NKJV) There are many scriptures in Matthew 6:25-34 that also support this belief system. The argument says that because the scripture says "need," it is clear that the Lord is only interested in meeting our needs and is not interested in our wants. In fact, many have the belief that wants are somehow frivolous. To be a spiritual person, frivolous things—even the desire to want something that is not a bona fide need—is a sure sign of being "worldly."

Another way of thinking, or the other side of the ditch, is the belief that you show your spirituality by how many wants you can amass. The flagship scripture for this belief is in 3 John 2: *"Beloved, I pray that you may* ***prosper*** *in* ***all*** *things and be in health, just as your soul prospers."* (NKJV) This argument states that God wants us to prosper, and being prosperous means whatever you want, you can have. Neither one of these beliefs are balanced, and both are akin to being in a ditch. In fact, I've heard it said that the devil doesn't care which side of the ditch you are in, just as long as you are in one. When you are in a ditch, you can't really go any where in life. We will never fulfill our purpose when our life is out of balance.

Both these beliefs on needs and wants have a very different perception of who God is. The "need-only" group perceives God to be frugal, cheap, and that He doesn't want His children to enjoy any of the pleasures of life. The other "as much of whatever you want" group perceives God to be a genie, a sugar daddy, and whatever-you-want type of father. God is neither of those perceptions. The God of the whole Bible is good, holy, and just. He wants His children to be well cared for and blessed. He is not cheap. He is not simply pragmatic. Look at this wonderful world He created for us! It is so incredibly diverse and so beautiful. If all He really cared for was just need and need alone, the world would not be so diverse and truly beautiful. He could have simply made it drab and boring, because after all, we don't need to look at a breathtaking mountain range, or to walk on the white sands by the seashore, or to wake up to an incredible sunrise, or to sit on a porch and watch the sun set while the sky becomes a pallet of more colors than you can dream of. We don't need those things to live. We just need water and food and a place to sleep. On the other hand, His blessings do not come without responsibility on our part.

There is a scripture in the Psalms worthy of thought: *"Trust in the LORD, and do good; Dwell in the land, and feed on His faithfulness. Delight yourself also in the LORD, And He shall give you the desires of your heart. Commit your way to the LORD, Trust also in Him, And He shall bring it to pass. He shall bring forth your righteousness as the light, And your justice as the noonday."* (Psalm 37:3-6, NKJV) This scripture is really thought-provoking. The psalmist says that God will give us the desires of our heart. You can look at this from an end-result perspective; in other words, you desire something, and God grants the desire. This is a valid interpretation as long as a person's desires are balanced and not driven by mere selfishness. However, there is another equally valid way to look at this. It is from the initiation perspective; the desire, itself, was first placed in your heart by God. This scripture also points out the balance that is found when we place our *entire* trust in the Lord. A person committing their life to God is not merely selfish and acquiring things for the sake of proving their spirituality. Nor will one flaunt their spirituality by having no material things that may bring any sort of pleasure in life.

Scripture is clear that God will bless His children with more than just provision for their needs. Abraham, David, and Joseph are just a few of the examples where God richly poured out His blessing in their life until their needs *and* their wants were combined. However, every one of these examples is of people who lived life in a balanced way. They understood their purpose in life, and their blessings in no way defined who they were. Their identity and worth was not found in their possessions; their identity and worth was found in the fact that they were children of God. They possessed things, but the things did not possess them. Trying this in your own life will change your perspective on your choices as a consumer. Find your identity in something greater than yourself and something greater than your stuff. With this attitude, your choices will be more directed at creating true value and you can enjoy your possessions without being identified by them.

On a Rock: Your Choices

The second building block for your solid financial foundation is your choices as a consumer. The way you analyze value and determine your needs and wants will influence your level of giving, spending, and savings. Life is not a series of circumstances; it is a series of choices. No one wakes up one morning to find themselves in financial trouble. Conversely, building a solid financial foundation will not happen accidentally. Deciding what you spend on wants and needs must be rationally analyzed.

You can choose value by remembering some simple principles. First, the greater your disposable income, the more resistant you are to financial crisis. Overspending for wants can complicate your finances. Overspending for needs can be financially ruinous. Next, your level of spending on wants and needs must be based on your income. You shouldn't be satisfied with your income, but you should recognize the types of spending you can do with the amount of money you make. Finally, purchasing value helps you stretch your finite money. Most people could live fulfilling and financially secure lives just by cutting out the junk.

The choices you make as a consumer are foundational to your finances. Your income will determine the level of your choices. The consumer choices you make will determine the amounts you can give, spend, and save to complete your financial foundation.

Your solid financial foundation:

- Income
- Choice

4 Your Giving

A wise man in a small town teaches his eldest daughter the importance of hard work and earning. Like all lessons difficult to explain in words, this man teaches with actions. He establishes a small lawn care business where once a week, his daughter can rake the leaves for five dollars per yard. The daughter dutifully grows the business to five yards earning twenty-five dollars per week.

The first Sunday, with twenty-two green dollar bills and three dollars in assorted small coins, the man teaches his daughter a second lesson: a lesson on giving.

"A tithe is ten percent of everything you earn that you give to the church. God requires we tithe," the man explains to his daughter.

So the daughter, who is mathematically adept, counts out two green dollars and two shiny quarters. The man smiles temporarily with the pride of a father, but as the Sunday proceeds, he realizes he has taught his daughter only the first directive of giving.

The next week, the daughter rakes the five yards and earns another twenty-five dollars. This Sunday, the father expounds on the concept of giving.

"Tithe is just the beginning of giving. God wants us to give more money than just the tithe. This is called an offering."

The daughter ponders this new advice. She has worked hard for her newfound wealth, but she also respects her father and wishes to please him. So she counts out two dollar bills, two shiny quarters, and one penny. She places the $2.51 of her tithe and offering in the collection plate. The father is discouraged with his teaching.

After church, he talks with his daughter, "Do you really think God is pleased with your offering?"

The daughter responds, "But you told me to give more than just a tithe. If my math is right, my tithe would be $2.50, so $2.51 is more than a tithe; just like you said."

The man smiles as the little girl defends herself with his words. "I'm afraid you misunderstood the basis of giving. Tithe and offering are not just about how little of our money we give away. When you give, God wants you to be generous and happy about giving. If you give grudgingly, it is as bad as not giving at all."

"But Daddy, I gave just like you said. I tithed my ten percent plus an offering," the little girl replies.

"But you gave your money away like this is the last twenty-five dollars you will ever have. If you tithe and share your blessings with others, God will bless you with more, first to bless others again, but also to see your abundance grow. God is not stingy to you. Why should you be stingy with the money God gave you?"

The daughter thinks for a moment, "Even if I work for it, and you pay me, it's God's money?"

"Everything we have on this earth; the sun, our food, your health, ultimately comes from God."

"Okay, Daddy, I will try to be more generous."

The man smiles. He prays that his daughter will understand this insight, and he thanks God, as most parents do, for an answer to a difficult question.

The next week, the daughter rakes leaves in the five yards again. On Sunday, the man and his daughter return to church. As the collection plate is passed by, the girl counts out two green dollar bills and two shiny quarters. The man holds the plate in front of his daughter to coax more money out, but she just smiles at him. The man is crushed; thinking his words have had no impact.

After church, the man talks to his daughter to correct her again. "I thought you were going to try to be more generous. I only counted two dollars and fifty cents. I thought you were going to do more than tithe."

"Well, I thought about what you said. And Mrs. Anderson has had such a hard time since Mr. Anderson died, so I raked her yard for free. I took ten dollars to the food drive at school, and I used five dollars to buy some cotton gloves for my friends who didn't have any. I gave half of what was left at church and put the other half in my piggy bank. You said that God knows about my wants too, didn't you?"

The man was stunned and silent. He absorbs the lesson that his daughter has just taught him. "Well done," he smiles as he hugs her. "Good job, Sweetie!"

Everyone understands generosity. Even if you are not a generous person, someone else's generosity has touched your life. Generosity takes many forms. Helping a mother with more children than hands, making a meal for the bereaved, or sparing some clothing for those who are without. Generosity is not just revealed in our financial giving; generosity is revealed in every aspect of our lives. A generous spirit can be revealed in something as small as a smile, or as note worthy as a multi-billion dollar endowment. Generosity is not just about what we give, but is more about how we give.

In the epistle that Paul wrote to the Corinthians, he pointedly stated what the father was trying to convey to his daughter: *"So let each one give as he purposes in his heart, not grudgingly or of necessity; for God loves a* ***cheerful*** *giver."* (2 Corinthians 9:7, NKJV)

Giving is more about the attitude of our heart than it is about the math. In fact, our attitude brings about the blessing that is directly tied to giving. We can easily do the math; the tithe is a tenth, so just move the decimal point to the left one number. Determining a mathematical amount for an offering is equally easy. Paul told the Corinthians, "*as he purposes in his heart.*" The question then becomes what kind of heart; a stingy heart or generous heart? The scripture states that God loves or delights in a giver with an attitude of cheerfulness. In other words, a person with a stingy heart most likely will not have a cheerful attitude. People like this are described as being "tighter than bark on a tree." That is the description of a stingy-hearted person. On the other hand, a person with a generous heart gives with joy. Cheerfulness is part of their giving. This is the kind of attitude God loves. It is the attitude the father developed in his daughter; it is also the attitude God wants us to have. It is this attitude that brings His blessing.

Parents understand this concept well. When our children do something we ask cheerfully, it just warms our hearts with a healthy pride. On the other hand, when they simply meet the requirements of obedience and are mad or frustrated while doing it, we are not proud of their effort. When our children obey cheerfully, it opens up other avenues of responsibility and trust given to them by us as parents. The opposite is true when done with a stingy effort. Even though a project is accomplished with both attitudes, the outcome or blessing is drastically different.

God, as our Heavenly Father, loves us and desires for us to develop and maintain a generous heart. He responds accordingly with increased trust and responsibility that ultimately translates into His blessing. Adopt an attitude of living to give.

A Bigger Piece of the Pie

People typically view their finances from one of two perspectives. The first type sees money as a pie. Because they see it as a pie, there is a finite amount of wealth in the world. This type of person will then jealously guard his piece of the pie. The person with a "pie" mentality views life from a totally limited perspective, and therefore life has only limited possibilities. From a financial viewpoint, he believes that for his wealth, or his piece of the pie, to get bigger, someone else's piece of the pie must get smaller. Giving, for this person, will always be limited by the nagging thought that their piece of the pie is getting smaller. A person with this perspective will not develop a generous heart. Despite this perspective being predominate in our society, this finite view of wealth is not only inaccurate, but it also creates a selfish and stingy heart.

The more generous and life-giving perspective views money as a river. Water merely flows through a river. In the same way, money flows into the river through various tributaries like wages, blessings, and profit. The money then flows out by way of expenses, spending and investments. The more money flowing in, the more money can flow out. Giving is another way that money can flow out. With this view, a person's wealth does not increase or decrease because of someone else's wealth accumulation. A person with a "river" mentality sees life with limitless possibilities. This person will give generously, with the knowledge that more money will flow in to them. They don't see the money they have as the last they will ever get. They don't live in fear that their pie is getting smaller with their giving because there is always the potential for money to flow in.

They give knowing they can earn more money, or their investments will return interest or profit. They are not constrained by the fear of not getting their piece of the pie. Seeing life as a river creates a generous and life-giving heart.

Getting a Blessing or Being a Blessing

We live in the most abundant and most fruitful country on the planet. When compared to other times or other countries, blessings truly abound. The middle class in America live more opulently than the rich of former years, or much of the rich in third world countries. In America, we should understand the concept of being blessed.

Many Christians confound what it means to be blessed. They will marvel when someone gives them a twenty dollar bill, but a job earning $2,000 every month is a burden and not viewed as a blessing. They think it is the blessing of the Lord when the clerk at the store rings their purchase up wrong saving them a few dollars, but a word of gratitude is never spoken for their good health, food, transportation, and shelter that they enjoy day in and day out. Blessings can be spectacular, but blessings flow into your life everyday in a less spectacular fashion. From the sun coming up in the morning, to your job, to the abundance at the grocery store, you are blessed every day. You are blessed whether you acknowledge and thank God for that blessing or not. However, acknowledging the many less-spectacular blessings we receive daily will keep our heart focused on being thankful. This will also encourage us to live with a generous heart.

While being blessed is satisfying, being a blessing to others is the essence of purposeful living. Being a blessing is the first step in fulfilling the purpose God has for us. In Genesis, God tells Abraham He will bless him to be a blessing: *"I will make you a great nation; I will* ***bless*** *you And make your name great; And you shall be a* ***blessing****."* (Genesis 12:2, NKJV) Abraham acquired great wealth and became the father of a great nation. You may think to yourself, if God gave me that type of abundant blessing, I too could use it to bless others. So what if you *do* have a blessing greater than or equal to Abraham's?

By living today in this country, you are probably blessed with more wealth than Abraham. Most likely, you live in a substantially larger home than Abraham. Your wardrobe consists of many more changes of clothing than Abraham most likely ever had. Your materials are finer and the weaving much more distinctive. Your home is furnished like a king compared to the wealthy man Abraham. Your transportation, regardless of how basic today, is more luxurious and comfortable than that blessed to Abraham. Abraham, as a wealthy man, endured times of hunger, but you claim hunger if you are thirty minutes late for a meal. You have access to health care, communications, transportation, and comforts that Abraham's Godly mind would have never imagined. If you had the same blessings as Abraham, would you try to be a blessing to others? What if your wealth *is* greater than Abraham?

Being a blessing seems contingent upon getting your finances in order. If you are in a season of your life where you barely make ends meet, it is more difficult to give. With a spirit of generosity, a "river" mentality, and the perspective of how blessed you are, you must reevaluate your obligations, debt, and spending. You will be given more specific tools in later chapters, but first you must develop a generous spirit and a willingness to fulfill your purpose in life.

Where do you start?

So how can you be generous until your finances are in order? First, we should give from what we have. Moses felt inadequate and overwhelmed when God asked him to lead the children of Israel out of their bondage in Egypt. You may feel overwhelmed by the bondage of your finances. Take heart. God asked Moses to use what he had at his disposal. Moses then used what he had, specifically the rod, to do mighty miracles and became one of the world's greatest leaders. You already have enough to grow to something great.

Remember, financial generosity is only a part of being generous. To practice generosity, give away your time and talent to people and organizations with more need than resources. Be free with friendly gestures and smiles. Be generous with advice and mentoring. And organize your life so you can give more financially, and give of yourself more easily. Because we live in a society that can be self-centered, creating and developing a generous heart can be difficult at first. The more you work at it, the easier it will become.

Philanthropy

The notion that the more you have, the more generous you become is not always true. The skills required to amass great wealth are completely separate from the willingness to give it away. While most of the extremely wealthy give away a lot of money, they have that type of wealth to give away. A percentage of the very wealthy give away as much of their wealth as they can, but that is a very small percentage. Most of the very wealthy give away less than ten percent of what they earn. Researchers have found that some money can buy happiness or pleasure resulting from what some material things can provide, but enormous sums of money cannot buy happiness. The researchers found that as incomes rose from $10,000 to $50,000, measurable happiness rose substantially. As earnings rose from $100,000 to $5 million though, money had no measurable impact on happiness. So if money can't buy happiness, why don't they give more away? Quite simply, it is because money doesn't buy generosity either. A generous spirit must be developed separately from the ability to financially give.

A man worth well over five billion dollars is considering a $105 million dollar gift to help build a new library at a local university. He meets with a university fund raiser at a café next to campus. As they dine on simple deli sandwiches, they discuss the transaction.

"So if I give $105 million, you will name the library after me?" the wealthy man asks.

"Yes," the college official replies, "I believe that is what we agreed to."

"What about $90 million," the man asks, "If I give $90 million would I still get my name on the library?"

"Quite frankly, sir, our fundraising has essentially dried up. Without that last $15 million, the library project will most likely be scrapped," the fund raiser explains. "So I guess, no. There would be no library to put your name on."

The two men discuss the specifics of the library and the gift. As they finish their conversation, a waitress politely and quietly clears the plates from the table.

"May I get anything else for you?" the woman asks with a smile.

"Just the check," the wealthy man grumbles.

She reaches in her apron and pulls out separate checks, both totaling $9.50. "Thank you for coming in," she smiles again. "Come again soon."

The wealthy man reaches in his wallet and pulls out a ten dollar bill. He places the bill and the invoice on the table. The fundraiser, similarly, places fifteen dollars on his side on the table.

"Is that University money you are giving away to that waitress?" the wealthy man asks. "Will my money be spent so casually?"

"Well, sir, it is my money. And five dollars and fifty cents means much more to that waitress than to me. As a matter of fact, I know that waitress. She is a part time student at our university. Her husband was tragically killed, and she is struggling to raise two kids. She works two jobs to pay for school and living expenses. This money that I so casually give away will make some difference in her life. She, I'm sure, is grateful for the fifty cent tip you gave her. But in her life, your stingy tip is as insignificant as your name on the library."

Jesus explains a generous spirit when He was in the temple at Jerusalem. He watches as rich people put their gifts in the collection box. A poor woman comes by and gives two small coins. Noticing the act, Jesus says, "Assuredly, this poor woman has given more than the rest of them. For they have given a tiny part of their surplus, but she, poor as she is, has given everything she has."

In this passage, Christ is not suggesting we give everything we have. Instead, He is explaining the concept of generosity. When you give to the church, the poor, the sick, the homeless, or the hungry, don't just give out of theological obligation; give with a generous heart. Giving isn't just about fulfilling the law or some religious tradition; it is about fulfilling genuine needs in other people's lives.

A person with a generous spirit will give even when the world scoffs at them. "I pay taxes, so the government can take care of the poor." "If they weren't so lazy, they'd have their own money." "My pastor offended me with his sermon, so I won't tithe." We have all heard these excuses, and many have heeded them. A generous spirit will ignore the skeptics and be a blessing in others' lives knowing that this is part of fulfilling their purpose in life.

The Instruction and Blessing of Giving

Tithing should be a familiar concept to those who have a Christian background and foundation, but maybe unfamiliar to those without such a background. The Old Testament book of Malachi gives us the underpinnings of tithes and offerings:

> *Bring all the tithes into the **storehouse**, That there may be food in My house, And try Me now in this," Says the LORD of hosts, "If I will not open for you the windows of heaven And pour out for you*

> *such blessing That there will not be room enough to receive it.*
> *And I will rebuke the devourer for your sakes, So that he will not destroy the fruit of your ground, Nor shall the vine fail to bear fruit for you in the field," Says the LORD of hosts;*
> *And all nations will call you blessed, For you will be a delightful land," Says the LORD of hosts.*
>
> *Malachi 3:10-12* (NKJV)

The word "tithe" means one-tenth. To tithe of your finances means to give one-tenth of your finances. The word "storehouse" in the above scripture, in modern usage, implies the "church." An "offering" is different than the tithe. An offering is given above and beyond the tithe, as we learned from the story of the father teaching his daughter about giving.

For the Christian, obedience in the area of tithing is foundational to living the Christian life. Giving offerings and almsgiving is cultivated by creating and developing a generous heart. A very powerful scripture in the book of Proverbs talks about a generous heart: *"The liberal **soul** shall be made **fat**: and he that watereth shall be watered also himself."* (Proverbs 11:25, NKJV)

Here it says, "the liberal soul." This is the same as saying the generous person shall be made "fat." "Fat" here is the same as saying they shall be blessed. The same thing is said in the second phrase. The New Testament talks about the same idea from another angle: *"Do not be deceived, God is not mocked; for whatever a man sows, that he will also **reap**."* (Galatians 6:7,

NKJV) The Apostle Paul tells the Galatians that we must always be aware of this precept. We will reap what we sow. This is also referred to as the "Law of Genesis." Apple trees produce apples, not green beans. Horses produce horses, not pygmy goats. When a person sows generosity, they will reap generosity. The same holds true for stinginess.

These scriptures reveal the truth that the blessing of the Lord rests upon those who are givers, both of tithes and offerings. His blessing rests upon those that have a generous heart. To walk in the blessings that the Lord has available for us, we must have this area of our lives in order and settled. Once we do, be ready for the windows of heaven to open up to you.

On a Rock: Your Giving

To many people, giving their money away seems counterintuitive from a financial perspective. How can you get ahead financially if you just give it away? Money that could be used for spending or saving? People with this attitude need the perspective that giving provides. As a building block to your financial foundation, charitable giving serves a financial purpose and a spiritual purpose.

From a financial standpoint, your money is not a solid financial foundation. Your actions and values in the use of money is the foundation. First, charitable giving acts as a buffer. Remember from the previous chapter, the greater your disposable income, the more resistant you are to financial crisis. Giving will instantly shift a substantial amount into disposable income. You will get in trouble financially if you always spend everything you have. The problem is even worse if your spending becomes obligated. Giving is the first step in adding a cushion between your income and spending.

Second, charitable giving will give you perspective on your money. Money and stuff is a poor reflection of your values, but giving clarifies what is truly important. Giving to a homeless shelter, to those suffering a disaster, or to a food bank will remind you how mild your money issues are.

From a spiritual standpoint, charitable giving is the most foundational aspect of your money. Simply by living in this country at this time, you are richly blessed with abundance. You should recognize this blessing and show your gratitude through your giving. Charitable giving will also open you to more blessings. When a person sows generosity, he will reap generosity. When he sows stinginess, he will reap stinginess.

You may be genuinely struggling with your finances. Chapters 5 and 6 will help you structure your spending to free up some more money for giving and saving. Until then, start by giving from what you have. Give generously of your time, talent, and your limited money. To tithe, give ten percent of your income to your local church. Determine your income, and move the decimal one place to the left. An offering is given above and beyond the tithe. (This equation and all equations are in the appendix at the end of the book.)

Charitable giving is the third building block to a solid financial foundation. Your income determines the level of your choices. The consumer choices you make will determine the amount you give, spend, and save. With charitable giving, you will recognize your abundance and prioritize your values. These prioritized values will shape your spending. Your savings will complete the buffer in your financial life that is started with your giving. But what will bind the financial foundation together? Keep reading to find out.

Your solid financial foundation:

- Income
- Choices
- Charitable giving

5 Your Planning

"How did I get here?" a person not too different from you sighs with frustration. "How did I end up in this mess?" he asks again. An average person may ask this question, and for the average person, the answer may look like this…

At some point, this person, let's call him Average Joe, enters the workforce. Whether after high school or after college, they earn a meager wage. Compared with no income, this new cash flow seems endless. When Joe should have asked, "How can I save my extra money?" he instead asks, "How can I spend all of this money?" It takes some thought, but Joe typically finds a solution to this money problem. He eats out as much as he can. He takes up a hobby like golf or snowmobiling. He tries some new pampering like massages or pedicures. As much as he makes, he spends it all.

As Joe becomes more comfortable with the steady flow of income, a car payment seems very reasonable. It seems pointless to live well and drive a jalopy. So Joe goes to a car dealer with the idea of purchasing a reasonable used car. At the dealership, the car dealer takes his income information, plugs it into a machine, and his credit score comes out. The salesman looks up from the paper with a smile and says, "With this credit score, you could buy that fancy sports car!"

Joe thinks twice about the sports car, chooses against it, but buys a nice new car instead of the used one, like he intended. He doesn't even ask the cost of the new car, he just makes sure he can afford the monthly payments.

With his new car, and the confidence of a wealthy man (that he really isn't), he starts dating. After several girls and several dates—all of them expensive—he finds true love. With true love, Joe purposes. He is told at the jewelry store he should spend two months of his salary on a tiny little diamond ring. He does the math quickly in his head and thinks about the boat or the trip he could buy with that much money. With the car payment, rent, and his lifestyle, it could take years to save that much money.

"Don't worry," the jeweler says with a smile, "we can set you up with a payment plan." With the excitement of a man who is about to propose, he buys the ring *and* the payment.

They enjoy a glamorous wedding and a regal honeymoon. Joe is surprised by all the gifts they get from their wedding; but is more surprised at all of the little things he and his wife buy. With the credit card payments from the honeymoon, he realizes life has changed and he needs to cut back. He has grown accustomed to his car, and he can't give up golf. He decides he will give up his massages and pedicures to make ends meet.

As the afterglow of the honeymoon wanes, Joe and his wife need a bigger place to live, so they decide to buy a home. They aren't sure how many kids they want, maybe five or six, so they buy a six bedroom, three bathroom house, just in case. They spend nearly forty percent of their monthly income on their house. These payments will become more reasonable once their income level increases. "It will get easier, won't it…won't it?" Joe realizes this is more of a hope and a prayer than a question.

First comes love, then comes marriage, then comes the baby and the baby carriage…and the car seat…and the diapers…and the medical bills…and the nursery…and the list goes on and on. The longer the list, the more money Joe spends. The bills and the debts pile up. Joe tries to readjust his life to reflect the change. He may give up golf. They may eat in more than dining out. Joe takes on more work and makes a little bit more money. But his payments for housing are still thirty-eight percent of his income. The utilities on a house that size really add up, too.

Joe's car is no longer practical. They need a new family car; maybe a mini-van or a station wagon. Joe is surprised at how little his car is worth. He is even more surprised at how much a family car costs. Can he really afford the payment?

Joe would give up other hobbies, but he has none. He feels like he works all the time and still can't make ends meet. His credit card debts are getting a little bit out of control and his home and vehicle eat up well over half of his income. After groceries and clothes, there isn't enough money to save for a rainy day. Maybe he could stop making insurance payments. Insurance…yeah, insurance payments.

This is where Joe really panics. Until now, the thought of a disruption in his life had never occurred to him. What if I need to meet a $1000 deductible on damage to my home or car? What if my car needs a major repair? What if I get sick? What if I lose my job? If I can't work, I will lose everything. Joe's heart is now racing as the "What ifs" race through his mind. "How did I get here?" Joe cried out, "How did I end up in this mess?"

Everyone could wake up one morning and "find" themselves in a similar situation. Even the wealthy aren't immune to this. They realize, too late, that buying the yacht and the summer mansion was too much. Regardless of your income level, if you spend all or more than your earnings, you will live pay-check to pay-check. So, how do you get out of this mess? Just like the mess wasn't created over night with one decision, it will take some time and a series of decisions to get out. You need to plan and prioritize your finances. The answer is simple; the action will take some time and dedication.

Planning by the Book

You have probably heard the well-known leadership quote, "If you fail to plan, you are planning to fail." There is a lot of truth to this statement. With financial planning, the average person feels inadequately equipped with the knowledge to do it successfully. Unfortunately, the average person is inadequately prepared or positioned to realize long-term financial success. So where do we start in the whole process? Let's first start by looking at what the Bible says about planning.

Jesus said that if we are going to be wise, we need to count the costs. Luke 14:28-30 says, *"For which of you, intending to build a tower, does not sit down first and count the cost, whether he has enough to finish it—lest, after he has laid the foundation, and is not able to finish, all who see it begin to mock him, saying, 'This man began to build and was not able to finish.'"* (NKJV)

Jesus says if we are to realize a goal, then we must plan a course of action to reach that goal. This particular scripture talks about a construction project. We really need to grasp and understand this principle He sets forth. Financial success that lasts the test of both time and any economic situation takes planning. We must *"count the cost"* of achieving the goal. Implicit in the principle is that sacrifice is necessary to reach the goal. For the average person, there is the sacrifice of not getting everything you want right now.

Delayed Gratification

Delayed gratification is a concept quickly becoming a relic of practical understanding and lifestyle behavior. The concept goes like this…I want something, but don't have the resources to acquire it right now, so I am going to plan a course of action to get the necessary resources. For instance, Little Johnny wants a new bicycle with all the latest bells and whistles, but doesn't have all the money needed. Mom and Dad have said if he wants it, he must buy it himself. So the gratification of having a new bicycle will be delayed until he has the resources to experience the gratification of owning a new bike. Little Johnny must now formulate a plan to somehow come up with the money to purchase the bike. He figures, or plans, that if he can mow 30 lawns during the summer, he will have saved enough to buy the bike.

Little Johnny will also pay tithes on the lawns he mowed, and will save the rest. With this plan, he will have enough money leftover to purchase the bicycle. His dad also suggests that he be generous by finding someone's lawn he could mow for free to give as an offering. So, he mowed the lawn of an elderly widow for free because he knew she was on a very limited income. The lemonade she gave him along with the heartfelt hugs made mowing her lawn more than worthwhile. At the end of the summer, Little Johnny mowed 31 lawns, paid tithes, and was diligent in saving the money. He goes to the store and buys the bicycle and has enough left to get an ice cream cone on the way home. Little Johnny delayed his gratification of owning a new bicycle for the time necessary to raise the money to purchase it.

In this scenario, Little Johnny learns an invaluable lesson that will set Little Johnny on a lifetime path of successful financial planning that he will also pass on to his children. Little Johnny *"counted the cost"* just as Jesus advocated in the New Testament. The gratification he felt by working hard, sacrificing time, giving, saving, and helping someone in need will benefit Little Johnny for the rest of his life.

Sadly, in today's financial culture, the story would be a bit different. Little Johnny would throw a fit and shame his parents into buying the bicycle, because every other little boy has the latest and greatest bicycle. Mom and Dad live from paycheck to paycheck and don't have the money set aside to buy the bicycle. But they don't want Little Johnny to feel like he is deprived, so they take Little Johnny to the store and get him the bicycle by putting it on a credit card. Little Johnny then rides the bike home so he can quickly get back to playing his video games for the rest of the summer. During a break in uploading a new video game, he uses his cell phone to inform all of his friends of his new acquisition. Growing up with that model of financial stewardship, Little Johnny grows up without understanding the concept of delayed gratification. His children and grandchildren also learn the same financial way of living only to find themselves at the mercy of the economy and every fad coming down the pike.

Planning by its very nature is just that....a plan. In other words, plans can change if necessary. Many people think that formulating a plan is somehow limiting. If you fall into that category, look at it from another perspective. See yourself as planning to succeed in your finances. Planning for financial success and security is not only doable, but absolutely necessary.

Solomon, who is referred to as one of the wisest men to ever live, gave an example of the ant to gain inspiration from:

> *Go to the ant, you sluggard! Consider her ways and be wise,*
> *Which, having no captain, Overseer or ruler,*
> *Provides her supplies in the summer,*
> *And gathers her food in the harvest.*
> *How long will you slumber, O sluggard?*
> *When will you rise from your sleep?*
> *A little sleep, a little slumber, A little folding of the hands to sleep—*
> *So shall your poverty come on you like a prowler, And your need like an armed man.*

Proverbs 6:6-11 (NKJV)

This portion from the Proverbs is applicable to our finances. The ant is proactive and doesn't wait until the last moment to gather food for the future. The ant does not live by the seat of her pants the way many people approach their finances. Most of us have probably done this. While we are young and fresh out of high school, we do not think about our elderly years. We don't think about the Biblical admonition to leave an inheritance to our grandchildren (Proverbs 13:22). We are basically concerned for the moment and acquire all the gadgets that make us cool and up-to-date. However, some forethought or planning would pay incredible dividends….literally! Countless people hit the panic button when their children start their own lives and they suddenly realize that they are behind the eight-ball in their finances. They have lived from paycheck to paycheck for so long that the slightest economic downturn has huge consequences to their ability to ride out the storm. The stress that this causes has profound consequences to their quality of life in every realm.

If we would heed the words of Jesus and Solomon, we can truly live with the peace of knowing we have a plan that will provide for our financial security. We will also leave a real inheritance to our children and grandchildren, as the Bible teaches us. Unfortunately because of a lack of financial planning, people can only pass on to their children and grandchildren a box of old photographs. A lifestyle of financial planning will have positive generational effects. We will model to our children, who will model to their children to financially plan for success.

Putting it all together

From a spiritual perspective, planning is key to charitable giving and living a purposeful life. With a plan, we will find a balance between our needs, our giving, and fulfilling our purpose. This life of balance is based on tithing a tenth of our financial increase, adopting a generous heart in all of our giving, and planning for our future. This strategy allows us to successfully survive and even thrive when we inevitably experience financial pressure because of the economy or the consequence of decisions we may make. A solid financial foundation does not occur by accident, but is the result of prayerful planning.

Planning by the Numbers

Everyone has a process by which they spend their money, and everyone has a means of prioritizing their spending. All people frame their financial decisions either emotionally or rationally.

Most of us know the person who makes emotional or temporal financial decisions. Their spending is very reactionary. They are sad, so they will buy something to pick them up. They are excited, often by a marketing advance, so they spend more than they need for an item. They are temporarily consumed by greed and see their resources as unrealistically limitless. Or perhaps this person, one that we all know, may make financial decisions based on fear. We will buy something as "for a limited time only," based on the fear it may no longer be available. We will buy more insurance than our life or property is really worth based on fear. We will buy virtually anything if an astute marketer can play on our fear and make us feel more secure with a product or service. Fear as a motivator causes overspending on items that make us feel safe.

The reason most of us know this person is because it is this person's reflection we see everyday in our mirror. We all have emotions, and our emotions make us uniquely human. Almost every marketer or advertiser appeals to their customers' emotions. They know you will buy things you don't need or even want, you will spend more than the items are worth, and with any skill, they will even make you feel good about your purchase. Most financial mistakes are made when emotions rule our decisions.

Instead, when we make our financial decisions based on prayerfully planned thought, our true priorities will shine through. In Matthew 6:21, Jesus says, *"For where your treasure is, there your heart will be also."*

(NKJV) When we spend without a plan, we will spend our treasure on things that will not fulfill our purpose in life. When you plan your spending, saving, and giving, you can prayerfully prioritize your life. If you stick to your plan, then your money will reflect your priorities and your true values. Remember, faith is the currency of heaven, and belief and action are the two sides of that coin. To ensure your financial actions match your beliefs, you must plan and prioritize your financial life. The most effective way to plan with prayerful thought is to plan with a pencil and paper in hand. Writing it down forces you to think about your income, priorities, and ultimate spending.

Step One: Create an Income Statement

In determining your financial plan, your income is the primary factor in your spending, saving, and giving. The only way to make a plan work is to first know what is flowing into your river. Your income statement is simply a list of the income you reasonably expect to receive. For most people, the number is the amount of after-tax wage that you receive. Using your after-tax wage simplifies your plan when you list expenses without a line for taxes. List your spouse's after-tax income along with any other income. This can include distributions from a trust, interest payments, payments from an annuity, payments from a legal settlement, payments from the government, or any income from a second job or other enterprise.

Determining your income is more difficult if your income is more variable. If your income is based on tips, commissions, overtime, or if you own a small business, you must carefully consider what your income truly is. With such variability, you should always estimate on the lower end of your historical income. As you allocate your income, the more cushion you have built into your plan, the more likely you will avoid a crisis. If you underestimate your income, once the money is earned, you can save it, give it away, or fold it into next month's budget. However, when you overestimate your income, a bad month at work will be amplified by a bad month at home.

With a variable income, you should also temper your success. Just because you have a good month or a good year, don't assume you can parlay that into more success. Many successful people have created financial instability in their lives. When they make purchases or acquire payment plans under the assumption of greater future income, if that income never materializes, then there will be a shortfall. The same is true for any anticipated income. An implied bonus, expected sales increase, or anticipated raise must be included in a plan only when the money is actually realized.

As you complete step one, this is also an opportunity to reevaluate your income. To make the numbers work on a plan, your income must be the same as your outflows. To make this balance, you can either cut spending, giving, or saving, or you can increase your income. An analysis of your income includes considering options to increase your income.

Step Two: Estimate Your Current Expenses and Obligations

Have you ever given a child a twenty dollar bill? They become excited and with a big smile and a thank you, they are on their way to spend it. They have very little restraint in their spending. They will impulsively buy the first thing they see and the money is quickly gone. If they save any or give any away, it is before they begin shopping. Rarely do they purchase anything of real value.

When asked how they spent the twenty dollars, they will stare blankly at you as they recreate the experience in their mind.

"Um…I, uh, well…I bought this gadget at the electronics store," they will say.

"Well, how much did it cost?" you may ask.

"I, uh…well…I'm not sure."

"You didn't spend all of it on this trinket, did you?"

"Well, no. I only spent a few dollars."

"Then where did you spend the rest?"

"I'm not sure. I'll have to think about it."

Fortunately, we are no longer children. We spend consciously and track our spending to a certain degree. However accidental it might be, we typically have an accounting of where our money goes. If we don't keep track intentionally, then you can recall purchases from a credit card statement or a bank statement. From this information, you can estimate your current expenses and obligations.

First, list your basic needs. Your list should include food, clothing, housing, health care, and transportation. Separate dining out from grocery purchases to better evaluate food costs. Your housing expense will include rent or mortgage payment, taxes, homeowner's or renter's insurance, repairs, and utilities. Health care can include any health insurance premiums, doctor or hospital care, medicines, and supplements. Your transportation category will include a car payment, auto insurance, fuel, maintenance and repairs, and any spending for public transportation. When you tie expenses to a category, be thorough enough to tie all spending to that category. At this point, only focus on needs. We will address wants later.

Next, you will estimate your short term obligations. Obligations are spending that you have already promised to pay and payments you must make to maintain services. Some obligations have been categorized as needs, but must be identified as obligations. This includes mortgage payments, car payments, insurance, property taxes, credit card payments, memberships, and any other fixed monthly payment. You may also include utilities costs like cable, telephone, internet, heat and electric, and water and sewer. These obligations may be needs or wants, but they are steady demands and can be changed very little in the short term. Even for spending that you can try conservation techniques, like lowering your thermostat to sixty five degrees, most of these obligations will move very little in the short term.

In analyzing these obligations, all of them can change in the long-term. All of our wants that are also obligations should be carefully reconsidered. Memberships of any kind, any entertainment that comes with a monthly payment, and all consumer debt should be reconsidered. Many of these obligations can be canceled or paid off. The more discretion you have in your spending, the easier you will balance your spending with your earning.

If these obligations for your wants can be eliminated, you have more flexibility in planning and spending, and preparing for any income disruptions. If you lose your job, paying for a vacation you already enjoyed or a television you can't sell will seem very foolish. Maintaining that membership or subscription without any income will make balancing your spending much more difficult. You can and should still spend your money on your wants, but that spending should not become a monthly obligation.

In estimating spending for our wants, you should appropriately categorize them. First, remember that every need can have a want portion to it. Designer clothing, name brand foods, high dollar restaurants, and even your house can be more than you genuinely need. If your spending plan will not balance, you should reevaluate the extra spending you do to turn needs into wants. Strict wants are more easily analyzed. Wants will include all entertainment, travel and vacations, recreation, dining out, and most service related activities.

Service activities can be difficult to evaluate. Many services like plumbers, mechanics, electricians, and lawyers are difficult for us to competently complete. Many activities like lawn care, house cleaning, and laundry could be completed by your household. These may be and should be categorized as wants.

As we categorize and evaluate our wants, you must remember that wants are an important part of our spending. Not all of our wants should be cut from our spending, but we must be smart about how we spend on wants. We must have the income to justify the spending we do on wants. If you are budgeting as a man and wife, determining wants may be the most contentious part of the plan. Be honest with each other, though. There are some things that men do that women will never understand. Conversely, there are some things that women do that men will never understand. Just because you don't understand spending that is important to your spouse, it isn't a reason to cut that spending from the plan. However, it must be appropriately categorized as a want for evaluation. When the actual evaluation comes, understanding from both of you is important in determining the level you can spend. Open communication, love, and understanding are essential in crafting a spending plan to which you will both adhere.

From a strict numbers perspective, wants will be the simplest to cut, but will take a certain willingness to give up things we truly want. At this stage, though, just list your current spending on needs, wants, savings, and giving, and note which spending is obligated every month.

Step 3: Prioritize <u>Your</u> Outflow Categories

Everyone prioritizes their spending. If you want a shallow glimpse into someone's heart, look at their spending. "Where your treasure lies, there your heart will lie also."

We have all seen the person whose number one priority is himself. Some are obvious: The father that spends his time and treasure at the bar and can't pay rent; or the mother who trades food stamps for drugs while her children starve. But other spending is less obvious. What about the father who works ridiculous hours just so he can ego-centrically live in the biggest house on the block? Or the mother who spends more on her family's appearance than they spend on groceries? What about the parents whose main priority is their children? They spend every extra dollar they make on their children's temporal desires. There is nothing wrong with making children a priority, except when your children's self-centered priorities are financed through you.

There is nothing wrong with enjoying comforts in life. Just understand the proverb that Solomon wrote, *"The blessing of the LORD makes one rich, And He adds no sorrow with it."* (Proverbs 10:22, NKJV) Many people say that the "new this" and the "new that" is simply the blessing of the Lord. However, when digging a bit deeper, the "blessing" of everything new has them in debt up to their hairline and living on the verge of financial collapse. Solomon wrote the blessing of the Lord has no sorrow attached to it. No sorrow of worry about making the payments. No sorrow of worry about what happens if they lose their job. No sorrow of worrying about an economic downturn. Being so deeply in debt is not blessing; it is sorrow. The wise person will live within their means. Spending more than our income is dangerously close to living in deception. We must prayerfully and thoughtfully prioritize our spending.

As you develop this list, it must be your priorities. Your life and circumstance is unique. Your upbringing, values, and passions will shape your priorities. You are a unique person, and your list of priorities will be equally unique.

Prayerfully considering your priorities and writing them down is an essential step in matching your actions with your beliefs. When you spend based on whim and purposeless want, there may be some discrepancy between belief and action. You may believe your house is the cornerstone of your financial life, but you spend so much on clothes that you miss mortgage payments. Your true belief is expressed in your action. You may believe that saving for your child's education is the most important want you have, but you spend all your extra money on vacations, birthdays, and Christmas. Again, your true belief is expressed in your action. You may believe in Christ and the financial tenets of tithing and giving as expressed in the Bible, but you never have enough money left over to tithe or give to the needy. Your true belief is expressed by your action.

As you prioritize your spending categories, just list them at this point. Don't worry about inputting dollar amounts just yet, just focus on priority. As you prioritize, do your needs first, then focus on any savings or debt elimination, and then prioritize your wants last.

Step 4: Allocate a Dollar Amount for Each Category

Now that you have evaluated your income and spending, and have considered your priorities, this step brings your plan together. At this point, you should have three lists: your income, your estimated expenses, and your priorities. For this step, start a new and separate list.

To begin, write your total income at the top of your plan. Below that, list your prioritized categories. List your most important category first and your least important last. Listing your prioritized categories like this will help you focus on what is most important to you.

Next, you must allocate a specific dollar amount to every category. Determining the amount of the first budget will be the most difficult. At this point, play with the numbers and get a feel of how close your spending plan balances. If your monthly earnings meets or exceeds your monthly spending, you should have no problem tweaking your numbers to fit your priorities. If you spend more than you earn, then the process will be more trying, but more necessary. You know better than anyone that this way of living is unsustainable.

There are several considerations when adjusting your spending. First, there are many obligations and payments that cannot be lowered in the short-term. Lowering your mortgage payment without first talking to your banker will result in foreclosure. Most utilities fluctuate up and down, but often independently of your desires. Don't assume a reduction in utilities on paper that will be difficult to replicate in real life. For the categories that you have more discretion, have a realistic plan to decrease spending. If you want to spend fifty dollars less on dining out, and each dining experience is about twenty-five dollars, then you must cancel two of your typical outings.

Is It Really That Easy?

As you skeptically read about planning, you may ask, "Is it really that easy? I just pray about it, think about it, and write it down. This really solves all of my money problems?"

The simple answer is…no, it isn't that easy. Writing your spending plan down is an essential component to controlling your spending, but there is no special power in the spending plan. The real power in the spending plan is the process. As you plan, you look at your finances from a more strategic perspective. You can make decisions based on your values and priorities and not based on how much money you have at any particular time of any given month. The true power in this plan lies in making the hard decisions at one time in a deliberate manner. You drive the process; not fate, or timing, or just hope. While planning, you can ask for advice from a mentor, or pray about a money decision that we might not normally find the time for in the marketplace.

The next chapter will show you an example of how this process can be applied. We also find ways to control spending to make our spending plan balance. At the end of the next chapter, there is a test, so be prepared. We will use these steps to walk you through your own spending plan. With some prayer and thought, you will regain some control over your spending with your own spending plan.

On a Rock: Your Planning

The next building block for your solid financial foundation is your planned spending. As you know, spending is easy; but spending for true value, that is a blessing in your life, is much more difficult.

Controlling your spending has two primary components: Planning, which we discussed in Chapter 5, and the execution of the plan which is Chapter 6. It is true, planning sometimes can be cumbersome and take much of our valuable time. When we execute our plan, things always change and our plan is rendered useless. But is it really useless? A plan must be flexible and account for changes in our assumptions.

So then, what is the value of planning? In a crowded and loud marketplace, you will spend impulsively. Your emotions are tricked and exploited, and you will buy things that add no value to your life. This includes all purchases from canned food to cars, to a burger and fries, and to your insurance.

Planning allows you to use your brain instead of your fickle emotions to analyze your purchases. With planning, you can prayerfully consider the purchases that will be a blessing without a salesman barking at you.

Planned spending is the fourth building block of a solid financial foundation. Your income determines the level of your choices. The consumer choices you make will determine the amount you give, spend, and save. With charitable giving, you will recognize your abundance and prioritize your values. Your prioritized values are carefully considered in a written spending plan. The spending plan must then be faithfully executed and your savings will complete the buffer in your financial life. But there is something more that will focus all of you actions to work together. Read on to find where that focus is derived.

Your solid financial foundation:

- Income
- Choices
- Charitable Giving
- Planning

6 Your Spending

How Average Joe Plans His Spending

To better understand the planning process, let us explore an example. Average Joe is an average man, with an average wife and an average 2.2 children. He has an average job and his spending is, you guessed it, average. Like the average person, Joe has very little in savings, would like to give more to charity, and has some goals bigger than the money he has left over at the end of the month. Joe will use the four-step spending plan to free up some more money in his life.

Step 1: Create an income statement

Joe has a very steady, average paying job. He earns about $48,000 per year after taxes. Jane, Joe's wife, brings home about $12,000 per year with a part-time job. Their combined annual income after taxes is $60,000 per year or $5,000 per month from their combined salaries.

Joe writes down the following information on a sheet of paper.

Income

	Salary	*$4,000*
	Jane's Salary	*$1,000*
	Total	$5,000

Joe considers some other income generating opportunities, but decides $5,000 per month is enough to live on for now.

Step two: Estimate your current expenses and obligations

Joe digs through his bank statements and credit card bills to compile his list. Every month, he gets $100 of "walking-around cash" that isn't in the statements, but that is rarely spent on anything other than entertainment. Joe looks through the statements and all of his spending fits into the average spending categories. Joe lists the categories, and with some simple math, fills in the following table beginning with his needs. To the right of his expense column, Joe breaks out the obligated portion of his spending, marking these amounts with a star. For instance, his mortgage and homeowners insurance is $1,500 of the total housing expense, so he lists that separately with a star. About half of transportation is a car payment; again he marks that fixed amount in the right column. All of his utilities are fixed and $200 of his health care is a premium for some supplemental coverage.

Expenses

Housing	*$1,750*	**$1,500*
Transportation	*$ 900*	**$ 450*
Food	*$ 600*	
Clothing	*$ 200*	
Utilities	*$ 250*	**$ 250*
Health Care	*$ 250*	**$ 200*

Next Joe lists his other short term obligations. Joe pays $50 per month for a term life insurance premium. He also has $100 left to pay on a summer vacation.

Life Insurance	*$ 50*
Vacation Debt	*$ 100*

Joe has two general wants. Joe spends nearly $700 per month on entertainment. Joe spends his entertainment dollars in the typical places: the movies, cable TV, music on CD and downloads, concerts, sporting events, and other amusements. He also buys entertaining products like: DVD's, books, subscriptions, a wide array of consumer electronics, and recreational and sporting equipment. Before you scoff and pass judgment on Joe's spending, I encourage you to figure your own entertainment spending. Yours may be higher or may be lower; this is just average Joe. Joe has a big heart though, and he gives $200 per month to his church. Joe completes his expenses table with the final two categories.

Entertainment	*$700*
Charity	*$200*

Step three: Prioritize <u>your</u> spending categories.

Joe looks at his listed expenses, and is a bit surprised at what this statement is communicating about his values and priorities. According to his spending, Joe's most important item is his housing, followed by his transportation, and then his entertainment. Joe has always thought of himself as generous, but his giving is the least important according to his spending. Joe wonders if this is really how he wants to live. He decides he wants to make a change in this area, to consider tithing and giving a priority, so now he lists giving at the top of his list. Joe also commits to save more money to cover emergencies, to use for vacations, to buy a new car, or for any opportunity. Joe makes entertainment less of a priority in his life. Joe writes down his list and reviews it.

Tithe and offering
Savings
Housing
Food
Transportation
Health Care
Life Insurance
Clothing
Utilities
Entertainment

Joe sizes up his list. He shakes his head as he wonders how he can free up enough cash to give and save. As it is, he barely makes ends meet. But Joe is committed, and he will work toward his priorities one decision at a time. If prioritizing and planning were easy, then everyone would do it…right?

Step four: Allocate a dollar amount for each category

Joe looks at his three lists. He lists his priorities in a column and then pencils in some values. Joe's spending is well beyond his earnings, so he uses his eraser to par back his spending. It is not easy, and his priorities are not fully reflected, but Joe is headed in the right direction, and this is the best he can do for now.

Tithe and offering	*$ 650*
Savings	*$ 200*
Housing	*$1,600*
Food	*$ 550*
Transportation	*$ 850*
Health Care	*$ 250*
Life Insurance	*$ 50*
Clothing	*$ 150*
Utilities	*$ 250*
Entertainment	*$ 450*
Total	*$5000*

Joe develops his new spending plan with his wife's help. He explains the spending plan to his teenage children, and while they don't like it, they are at least informed.

Joe starts with just tithing. His before tax monthly income is $6,000, so a ten percent tithe is $600. Joe gives an extra $50, and wants to give above and beyond this, but Joe is tied up with his obligations. In the future, He will downsize his car which will generate some more income. Joe will allocate $200 per month toward savings for now, and this will go to his emergency fund. Then as Joe's spending frees up, he will devote considerably more to savings. Joe's spending plan includes savings of $150 per month by doing all of his own lawn care and home repairs. They will give up soda to save about $50 per month on food as a family. They will cut back on driving, and their clothing budget is dropped. They will spend nearly half on entertainment. They will adjust their cable package, cancel one of their two movie trips, and their kids won't have free reign at the mall. Joe looks at his list again. He is frustrated that his priorities aren't fully reflected in his spending, but he at least has a start. In the months to come, Joe will adjust his spending.

Value

As you look over Joe's spending plan, some things may seem absurd. Do people really spend that much on entertainment? Do you? What is even more absurd is the amount spent for "needs." Everyday people spend only a few dollars per day to cover their basic needs, but in America, covering our needs has become a competition. How much can we spend on our house? How much can we spend on clothes? How much can we spend on our food? But the question is: what are we *really* getting for the money we spend?

We must walk the fine line between living abundantly and living in excess. A key to walking that line is buying for value. We must get the most benefit from every dollar we can. As we select our consumer goods, whether it is as big as a house or as small as a soda, we must make our limited funds best meet our true needs and wants based upon our priorities. This is difficult in a society where billions of dollars are spent annually on marketing designed to get you to part with your money. In buying for value, you determine what is most important to you and your family and purchase it at a quantity and price that matches your income.

To illustrate this point, walk through your house, or your storage shed. Look at your bank statement and note all of the purchases you made that, in hindsight, really didn't fulfill a want or need in your life. Did you really need that treadmill? And how about the new professional set of cooking knives that slices and dices—

all for a special TV only price of $19.95 plus $8.95 shipping and handling? And for your kids, did they *really* need that video game that teaches them a set of values contrary to yours?

In a simpler time, it was a necessity to purchase value. The average person would spend most of their income on food, clothing, and shelter. Basic transportation was relatively inexpensive, but it was also very inconvenient. Health care did not consist of thousands of dollars worth of life saving procedures; the doctor could provide a simple cure, or you would die. In a simpler time, the average person had very little disposable income. It wasn't necessarily a better time, but it was a simpler time.

In an economy with as much choice as we have, marketers must differentiate their products. Marketers use techniques that can compel people to buy products they don't want or need, pay more than they intended, and then make them feel good about their purchase buy minimizing buyer's remorse. Don't get me wrong, marketers are not evil; they're just business men and women trying to make a buck like the rest of us. In an economy with as much disposable income as we have, marketers of both wants and needs must compete for those extra dollars. As a consumer purchasing value, you must determine what your wants and needs really are.

Just think of an average couple, let's call them Jack and Jane, as they go through the grocery store. As they walk through the door, they see a table of "sale" items. Are these really a bargain? Is something wrong with these products? Are they cheaper than normal? This is the first of hundreds of sale signs through the store.

As they walk through the aisles, they dig to find the items they really want, because the only items they can easily see are the ones the grocery store wants to sell. As Jack and Jane wander through all corners of the store to find products that should be grouped together, they see other products that are deeply discounted. Is this another sale? Some of these products are sold at or below cost. How does the store make money on these products? Don't worry, Jack and Jane…the store makes money.

At the back of the store, a nice woman prepares food and offers it to Jack and Jane for free. That is nice of the store, they think, but as skeptical consumers, they wonder what the store is accomplishing.

Jack and Jane spend more time than they want filling their shopping list, but they finally reach the checkout stand. Next, the barrage of questions begins. Would you like our featured product? Would you like to double this purchase for only half more? That really is a good deal. Would you…Would you…Would you? The clerk is very friendly with the questions, and Jack and Jane are very tempted to say yes.

Next comes the customer loyalty programs. Do you have our super-duper saver card? If you have one, you could save big. Would you like a store credit card? You'll save ten percent today with one.

As a bedraggled Jack and Jane walk out the door, they read the receipt. There is a 1-800 number to call with any problems. If you are unsatisfied, let us fix the problem. Jack and Jane are tempted to call, but they have already spent enough time with the store, and where would they start with their list of complaints.

What if Jack and Jane were given a special pair of glasses to see the sales techniques against them? With these glasses, they walk through the door and see a table with a big sign that says, "Sale of Things Nobody Else Wants! Yes the price is lower, but customers aren't buying even at the lower price." With their glasses, the other sale signs say things like, “Cheaper Prices Because We Bought Too Much,” or “Cheaper than the Original Markup,” “Sale…But Not Really Cheaper,” or “Cheaper Only Because We Need Room For New Product.”

“These glasses are very helpful,” Jack tells Jane.

With these glasses, Jack and Jane walk directly to only the products they need. Without the glasses, they wandered from aisle to aisle, looking at the entire product offering just to find what they really want. With the glasses, they avoid buying something they see but don’t want. They again see the deeply discounted product that, like before, is at or even below cost. Except with the special glasses, the product cautions that the store has extensive research to identify products customers buy together. The caution tells Jack and Jane that the peanut butter is deeply discounted, but the price of jelly, bread, and milk has increased to make up the difference.

“I always wondered how a store makes money by selling below cost,” Jack comments.

“Now we know,” Jane replies with a smile.

Jack and Jane again reach the back of the store where the nice woman gives away free samples, but this time they are wearing their special glasses.

“Would you like to try a free sample?” the woman asks. “We know that if you try something, you are likely to buy it. Just be glad it is a frozen pizza and not jewelry, clothing, or a new car.”

Jack and Jane smile politely, but they don’t nibble on the bait.

Remarkably, Jack and Jane quickly have a cart full of food they really want. They hurry to the checkout stand to face the barrage of questions; but this time they have their special glasses.

“Would you like to buy our featured product?” the woman asks with a smile. “Consumer psychologists have shown that most people have an aversion to saying 'no' to another human being."

"No thank you," Jack and Jane reply.

"Would you like to double this purchase for half the price?" the clerk asks again. "My employer insists I ask the full litany of questions."

"No thank you," Jack and Jane reply.

"Do you have a super-duper saver card?" the clerk asks. "If you shop here again and again, that is really where we make money. Or do you want our store credit card? Studies show you will spend twelve to eighteen percent more with a credit card than without. That is why we are happy to pay the fees associated with the card."

"No thank you…no thank you…no thank you," Jack and Jane are now robotic with their responses.

As Jack and Jane walk out of the store, they look at their receipt through their special glasses. The same 1-800 complaint line is there, but this time with a caveat. "We will do anything we can to get you to forget you buyer's remorse. If we convince you to buy things you don't need at prices higher than you're comfortable paying; we still want you to feel good about the experience. With your complaint, we can do damage control and make our marketing techniques even more subtle."

"That's interesting," Jack says. "I don't have buyer's remorse because we only bought what we want."

"Too bad we can't always have these glasses," Jane answers.

"Yeah…too bad."

The Art of Marketing

Marketers of all products and services will use some simple techniques to generate greater sales. This applies to *all* goods and services. Be cautious of these techniques when buying food, clothing, and consumer goods, because buying value on these smaller items can really add up. Many people can recognize these techniques; however, the greater the price, the higher the marketing stakes. Similar marketing techniques are used to sell cars, homes, insurance, banking services, mortgages, investments, health care, legal services, accounting and tax preparation, and almost every other professional service. You will even recognize these techniques employed by charities and advocacy groups.

Keep this is mind as you read some of these techniques. They are used at the grocery store and restaurant, but are also used by your realtor, broker, insurance agent, and lawyer. Some of these decisions can cost you tens of thousands of dollars. Be especially vigilant buying for value on these life-changing purchases.

Sale!

A local clothing store is having a clearance sale. A large yellow sign with big black letters promotes this sale. The sale goes on…and on…and on. This clearance sale last for years. The yellow sign fades and become tattered. After four years of "Clearance" the sign is no longer presentable. The sign finally comes down…and is replaced with a new yellow and black sign that reads "Blowout Sale!"

Consumers have a certain weakness for a sale. You may assume that sale means lower price or greater value. Not all sales are created equal. Sales *can* be a genuine bargain for a value seeking consumer; but you need to shop with your eyes wide open. Some sales liquidate merchandise by lowering price, while other "sales" are meant simply to increase traffic, without the benefit of a lower price. To take advantage, be price conscious and determine genuine bargains from just sales.

Most items have a seasonality based on either season of use, or based on the industry timing of new models. With some research, a consumer can determine when merchandise will be deeply discounted because of seasonality. This is the most predictable means for finding an authentic sale having true lower prices.

Promotions and Features

Promotions and featured items are often marketed in conjunction with an advertising campaign. These will be higher margin items with which the store will make a substantial profit per sale. These are simply items the store will introduce to you in their advertising. These are not sale items. It is the new model or a popular item that the store can mark up.

The consumer must use much caution with this type of marketing. Promotions and features are products or services that lead to a greater profit for a store; therefore, the store will want you to buy them. It is not necessarily something you really need, but may want. Deals can generally be found on these same products when their luster wanes and they are no longer new or hot.

The Loss Leader

With the loss leader technique, a store will lower the price of a product at or below cost. The store will lose money on the loss leader, but make up the money (and more) on a complimentary product. A classic example will sell drastically reduced peanut butter, but raise the price on jelly, bread, and milk. A store will sell a dress at or below cost but raise the price on matching shoes and accessories. The store does extensive research to find very subtle complimentary products.

The loss leader is annoying when it is employed for these small items. The loss leader can be financially ruinous when used with financial products. A mortgage company will use the loss leader. They will offer a mortgage with a teaser rate. The teaser rate will be very low and will entice the buyer. The mortgage company will break even or lose money until the teaser rate expires and the owner must pay the balance of the loan at a much higher rate. Credit card companies will also use the loss leader. A credit card will have a low interest rate which makes the company very little money. Once you create a substantial balance on the card, the company will raise the rate and impose fees and penalties that pad their profits; this is their loss leader strategy. They won't make much money until you pay at the new rates. The too-good-to-be-true rates they offer truly *are* too good to be true. What is profitable for them can be devastating to you financially.

Try It, You'll Like It

A man and his fiancée walk into a jewelry store. The woman excitedly looks at the selection, while the man is scared as he looks at the prices. The jeweler watches the potential customer like a vulture watches a dying rodent. If the woman hesitates slightly at a diamond ring, the jeweler quickly unlocks the case and places the valuable ring on the glass table.

"You are welcome to try it on," the jeweler says. "That is a lovely ring…try it on. That would look perfect on your finger, try it on. Try it on. Try it on."

If a salesman can convince a customer to try something, they will most likely buy it. Do clothing stores really want people wearing their inventory? Do car dealers really trust you with a $20,000 asset? They do because you are likely to buy what you try.

Is there a danger of trying a product you intend to buy? As an informed consumer, you should like the fit or how the product feels or tastes. Trying the product should be a step in purchasing, but it should not be the first step. Find an item you want and fits your spending plan, and *then* try it. Too many consumers buy impulsively once they try the product.

Monthly Payment Plan

"Six hundred dollars for a new dish washer!" the customer exclaims. "I can't afford that. Do you have a less expensive model?"

"But sir," the salesman rides into the rescue, "we offer a monthly payment plan. No interest for one year. You can afford $50 a month."

A consumer will spend more for an item if it can be broken down into an easy monthly payment. Most higher-priced items can be purchased this way. A store may even absorb the interest because you will spend more with a payment plan.

A store pays a fee to a credit card company every time you use a credit card. Why would a store pay a credit card company to process your transaction? Are they really that concerned about your convenience? When it comes to separating money from you, the more convenient…the better. Studies show the typical customer will spend twelve to eighteen percent more with a credit card than with a check or cash, so the store appreciates the convenience of a credit card much more than you do. A wise consumer searching for value will be skeptical of any program to make payment easier. Additionally, the more obligated your monthly income becomes; the more difficult it will be to balance your monthly spending plan.

The Leading Question

The leading question has become a well-known fast food restaurant cliché. "Would you like fries with that?" A typical customer will feel left out if he isn't asked about his fries or drink needs. So why do companies ask these questions? If I had wanted the fries, I would have asked for them, right? Not right. The leading question exploits the most vulnerable customer: the customer who has already committed to a purchase. The leading question takes advantage of simple human psychology. We have an aversion to say "no" to another human being. We will say "yes" to almost any mundane thing to avoid saying "no."

As a consumer looking for value, you should always buy what you want, and only what you want. Buying value does not include buying what the retailer wishes you to buy. If you still have an aversion to saying "no," then try saying, "no thank you."

More for Less

A retailer will often offer a deal that seems too good to be true. For just a little bit more money, you get so much more product. You can "supersize" your purchase for just a few pennies more. Often the seventeen-year-old economist behind the counter will question your logic when you pass up one of these deals. "It's only forty-nine cents more," they reason, "and you get all of this extra."

A smart consumer seeking value can use these deals to their benefit. If the quantity they want or need falls within this more for less quantity, then take advantage of the savings. However, the normal consumer will typically purchase and use the product in excess, and this causes two problems. First, you are buying at a quantity the store wants, and not what you want. Second, you will spend more on the item than you intended.

Like all purchases, falling for this technique for small purchases is a slow drain. With larger purchases, the drain is even faster. Insurance agents will do this effectively. "An extra $100,000 in life insurance coverage is only $20 more per month." "Full coverage for your auto policy is only $35 more per month." Many professionals will employ this technique to add services to the package. This technique is even more effective with a monthly payment plan. The "more" that they offer seems even more pronounced when the "less" is spread out over twelve monthly payments.

Customer Loyalty Programs

The most profitable customer for any business is repeat customers. A business will do almost anything to entice you back. The most useful means is through a customer loyalty program. If you have their card, you can save every time you come back. If you shop with them, then eventually you will receive some customer appreciation gimmick.

Customer loyalty should be earned every time you frequent a store. Customer loyalty is earned by offering the best value to a customer. It isn't a meaningless piece of plastic you carry in your wallet. It isn't a free gift for putting up with them for a few months. A consumer buying for value should be a loyal customer, but your loyalty should be as a satisfied customer and not based on a cheap marketer's trick.

Free

"Tanstaafl," the economics professor tells his class.

"Is that Dutch?" one student asks without raising his hand.

"No, no," the professor replies. "Tanstaafl is a long standing economics principle. Tanstaafl is actually an acronym."

The curious class is silent as they await the secret from their professor.

Almost whispering, the professor says, "Tanstaafl is an acronym for **T**here-**a**in't-**n**o-**s**uch-**t**hing-**a**s-**a**-**f**ree-**l**unch…Tanstaafl."

The economics professor uses tanstaafl to clarify his point about opportunity costs, but it applies even more to a consumer of value. Everyone has been seduced by the promise of free. Most of us have fallen for this ploy repeatedly. Whether it is a free drink with dinner, a free gift with purchase, or free frequent flier miles, the lure of free is strong. Whenever you see a business offer something for free, it never is. "Free" will always be attached with something else for a price. Sometimes the "for a price" portion will be very covert, but it will always be there. Understand the cost of the complete package, not just the free portion. A consumer buying for value will calculate the true cost of free. Always remember…Tanstaafl.

Customer Feedback

Everyone has seen "that" customer. If something isn't just like they want, they complain. If the resolution is unsatisfactory, they find a manager. If they are in any way unsatisfied, they will complain. The retailer will appease this customer in any way they can, because from the retailer's standpoint, the customer who complains is a good customer. Yes, you read that correctly...a good customer. The good customer will give the retailer a second chance to make things right. The good customer also helps the manager adjust their operations to better serve customers.

Conversely, a bad customer is one who smiles politely and never says a word. If they are unsatisfied, no one realizes. The bad customer will say "thank you" as they leave, will vow never to return, and will tell ten friends how bad their experience was. A store prefers the vocal customer that allows them to make things right and adjust their operations.

For a consumer buying value, there is nothing wrong with complaining. However, if you are always complaining about a product or service, then you must reevaluate its true value. Customer feedback also allows a retailer to minimize buyer's remorse. Buyer's remorse is an important tool of a value seeking customer. Buyer's remorse is the dissatisfaction a customer feels with a purchase they regret making. A consumer searching for value uses buyer's remorse to identify if a purchase is valuable to them.

There is a conflict between a customer and a marketer. The value buying customer will purchase goods and services they really want, at a quantity and price they are comfortable with. A marketer is selling their product offering at a quantity and price that maximizes their profits. This quantity and price may not be at the same level. A consumer searching for value must cut through the marketing and buy things they really want or need. This same philosophy is the foundation of an effective spending plan. You must spend your money on goods and services that satisfy a want or need in your life.

Make It Happen

Now it is your turn. The next several pages in this chapter should be studied with a pencil and paper in hand. We will walk through your spending plan, but you will need to write it down. You don't need a special form; you don't need expensive software; you don't need last year's tax return, and you don't need to hire an accountant. You just need a pencil and paper, and you just need to start.

1. Create an Income Statement

List your reasonably expected monthly income. This includes household wages after taxes, and any other steady monthly income. If your income is not steady or predictable, your income statement should be estimated low. If your monthly estimate is lower than actual, then you can carry over until next month. If your estimate is higher than actual, you will tap savings or use debt to balance your spending. Bonuses, tax refund and other one-time payments should not be anticipated. Once you have cash in hand, you can allocate it as an expense or savings.

2. Estimate your current expenses and obligations

First, estimate your basic needs and your short term obligations. If you don't have an accounting system, just use bank statements and credit card bill.

Basic needs:
Food, clothing, housing, health care, transportation. Remember to designate any fixed payments or obligations

Short-term obligations:
Any fixed monthly payment that is not all ready designated as a need.

Wants:
List how much you currently spend on your wants: entertainment, recreation, travel and vacations, and leisure and pampering.

3. Prioritize <u>your</u> outflow categories

This must be your list. Others can tell you what are important expenditures, but this must be your list if you expect to follow it. Don't worry about the dollar amounts yet, just focus on categories. People tend to set their priorities either emotionally or rationally; prioritizing with a pen and paper helps you to focus your thinking.

To help you prioritize:

<u>Needs first</u>:
Tithe and charitable giving
Taxes and legal obligations
Food
Housing (including mortgage, insurance, taxes, maintenance)
Health Care (including insurance & knowing it won't cover everything)
Clothing (understand the wants portion of clothes spending)
Basic utilities (some utilities are wants)
Transportation (including gas, debt, maintenance, & insurance)

Savings next:
Emergency Fund
Debt Payments
Goal based savings & investing
Other insurance (term life, disability, long-term care)

Wants last:
Entertainment
Travel
Dining out
Special events and occasions

4. Allocate a dollar amount for each category.

Now that your spending is prioritized, the next step is funding the categories. The needs should be funded according to your expense estimates. At this point, you should re-evaluate excessive spending on needs. Do you spend too much on name brand clothing? Do you drive more car than you need? Can anything be done about utilities, health care, or any of the other categories? Any reduction of expenses should be realistic. The wants are funded with what remains of the monthly income. If it is important to you, you should pay tithe, charitable giving, and savings first. The government insists that you pay taxes first for a reason: if it isn't first, you may not have enough left over at the end of the month to pay the full amount. The same can be said of tithe, giving and savings; if you only fund these categories with what is left over, then assuredly, you will rarely have any left over.

The Enemy

There are several factors that will prevent your spending plan from balancing. These factors are totally under your control and certainly drain your finances.

Debt. For many people, debt spending is the only way they can balance their current spending. This short-term solution will be a burden on your spending plan for months or even years to come. Any debt with compounding interest greatly hinders your ability to balance future spending plans.

Debt generally, and credit card debt specifically, will also alter the way you spend. The more difficult the transaction, the less likely you will complete it. Just like coins made exchange easier than barter, credit cards have simplified exchange. Most people will justify their credit card because of the ease of use, but this is the inherent problem. Remember, consumers spend twelve to eighteen percent more with a credit card, and the numbers are even more dramatic with internet purchases. The internet is a marketer's dream not only because of how consumers can be targeted and manipulated, but also because of the convenience of purchasing.

Debt for major purchases must be evaluated carefully to avoid tying up your spending plan. As a rule of thumb, your housing expense (including principle, interest, property taxes and homeowner's insurance) should be no more than 28% of your monthly after-tax income. If you want to be a steady giver, then your after-tithe income will be ten percent less. Therefore, you should spend no more than 25% of your after-tax income. This rule of thumb is a maximum, and if your payment is less, your spending will be much easier to plan. Total monthly debt payments should be no more than 36% of your monthly after-tax income. Again, adjusted for tithe, that number should be less than 32% of monthly after-tax income. The lower your monthly debt obligation, the more freedom you will have in your spending plan.

It is important to point out that debt in and of itself is not bad. Debt causes problems when it is out of control and rules a person's life. Some Christians feel that debt even reaches the level of sin by referring to the Apostle Paul's admonition to the Romans: *"Owe no one anything except to love one another, for he who loves another has fulfilled the law."* (Romans 13:8, NKJV) The context of the writing is about love, not a financial admonition. Part of the blessings of Abraham is that we be the lenders, and not the borrowers. *"For the LORD your God will bless you just as He promised you; you shall* ***lend*** *to many nations, but you shall not borrow; you shall reign over many nations, but they shall not reign over you."* (Deuteronomy 15:6, NKJV)

We want to live in the blessing of the Lord so that we are not bound by debt. Clearly, if debt were sin, then the blessing of the Lord in the scripture above would not make sense. God in no way would bless us so that we could be the cause of someone else entering into sin by lending to them.

Endeavor to live "debt-free." There is a freedom that can be experienced when we are not constantly wondering how to make ends meet. As we make wiser choices and get out of the maze of bondage debt can bring, there is a freedom and liberation you can experience. You will never get caught up in the bondage of debt again. Make money serve you, don't serve money.

<u>Monthly Payment Plan.</u> The monthly payment plan is the cousin of debt. Remember, the more discretion you have in your spending, the easier your spending plan will

balance. A monthly payment plan removes this discretion. If a membership or subscription is tied into an automatic payment plan, the seller worries you may not value the service as much in the future as you do when you impulsively subscribe. Stopping these payments in a crisis takes time, so don't put yourself in that position. There are also months where other expenses go up, and you are still committed to this payment.

Some people will justify a monthly payment plan as a good way to boost a credit score. This only works if you make all of the payments. It is a poor justification when saving that same amount can accomplish much more than a higher credit score.

<u>Overpayment of Taxes</u>. Some people get excited every April when the federal government gives them "free money." They never realize this is simply an interest free overpayment of taxes. They aren't giving you free money, they are giving you back money that always was yours. If your refund is over $800, you need to adjust your withholding by correctly filing a W-4 to reflect your tax situation. An extra $60 per month makes balancing your spending plan easier. It also removes the temptation to blow the lump sum that you get as a refund.

<u>Your children.</u> Your children should not dictate your lifestyle. As a parent, you have the wisdom and life experience that they haven't had time to develop. You are more mature, more responsible, and have the authority to care for them; but many parents simply turn over spending decisions to their children. Children hate being told no, but they crave boundaries and structure. From a spending perspective, this is a serious conflict. Your children may despise you in the short-term, and

think their pressing need is much more important than a solid financial foundation. One of the greatest gifts you can give your children isn't "stuff," but rather an appreciation for money and work.

Special Events and Occasions. Have you ever celebrated Christmas in March? Many people are still paying for Christmas in March. Christmas, Easter, and birthdays are special challenges for a spending plan. Vacations and almost any special event can be overspent. You can easily get caught up in the emotion of a special event, and when this happens, money is no object. Special events should be enjoyed, but they are more enjoyable if you don't worry about how you will pay. You may even complete a separate spending plan for any special event.

The Internet. The internet has taken spending convenience to a new level. Throughout history, when spending becomes easier, then consumers will spend more. The internet is a marketer's dream. Because every purchase is already digitized, there is very little cost to build a marketing database that can show trends, complimentary products, and pricing schemes. With cookies, internet retailers can profile you when you enter the site and tailor their marketing specifically to you. Additionally, the only way you can pay is with a credit card, and we have already established the problems with credit cards. The internet is a phenomenal informational gathering tool for an informed consumer. It is also a marketers dream come true.

On a Rock: Your Planned Spending

Planned spending is the fourth block to building a solid financial foundation. Planning is an important and simple step in controlling your spending, but the more difficult step is executing your plan. The faithful execution of your spending plan is imperative to maintaining your solid financial foundation. You will want to buy value at such a level to free up money for saving and giving. This chapter discusses the marketing techniques used to separate you from your money. Also discussed were the most common obstacles to maintaining a workable spending plan. This chapter is also a call to action. These ideas work best if you write your spending plan down. Ease your crowded brain by putting your thoughts down on paper.

Planned spending is the fourth building block of a solid financial foundation. Your income determines the level of your choices. The consumer choices you make will determine the amount you give, spend, and save. With charitable giving, you will recognize your abundance and prioritize your values. Your prioritized values are carefully considered in a written spending plan. The spending plan must be faithfully executed in a noisy marketplace. Finally, your savings will complete the buffer in your financial life. Chapter seven will explain how your purpose will focus your action and bind your financial foundation together.

Your solid financial foundation:

- Income
- Choice
- Charitable Giving
- Planned Spending

7

YOUR PURPOSE

Everyone is driven to accomplish something in their life. As you scoff and shake your head, you are certain that statement is false. Again, everyone is driven to accomplish something. You certainly have someone in mind that will refute this claim. Let us describe them.

Slacker is a twenty-four year old male. His real name isn't Slacker, but everyone calls him Slacker and it fits. Slacker lives in his mother's basement. Slacker has very few friends, and his interests are very narrow. He loves video games. He spends ten hours per day honing his skill on his gaming system. When Slacker isn't playing, he researches his games in a magazine or on the internet. He has conquered almost every game he has tried.

But Slacker isn't one-dimensional. Slacker has a "green thumb." He has an indoor hydroponics garden where he maintains fourteen plants. Slacker has thirteen marijuana plants and one tomato plant to keep his mother guessing. His sense of accomplishment courses through his body as he smokes his home grown pot and plays his video game. Slacker is passionate about his mindless video game and his mind altering drugs. His drive and accomplishment is devoted entirely to himself.

Let's describe another example of drive. An athlete is driven to be the best. From the time he was a small boy, he only thought about winning the championship. He works fourteen hours per day training his body and mind to perfection. He constantly yells at any of his teammates that aren't as driven as him. He is consumed with victory. He makes millions of dollars, but seeks only the glory of winning.

When the athlete finally makes it to the big game, he plays like a warrior. All of the work, all of the time he has put in comes down to this one game. Everything in his life comes down to winning. As the game goes final, the athlete tastes the ultimate victory. He cheers, he weeps, and he kisses the trophy. He toiled for twenty years to make this moment a reality.

Once the cheering stops, and the confetti is cleaned up, the athlete remains with his trophy. All of the effort, all of the drive, and the reward is a twelve pound hunk of metal. He weeps again, this time as he realizes his ultimate goal results in just this meaningless trophy.

So, you are not a slacker and not an athlete; but you are driven. There is *some*thing that drives you. It may be money; it may be a sense of responsibility, or maybe it's just the satisfaction of accomplishment. But, everyone has God-given abilities and passions accompanied with the drive to make them come to pass. The challenge is finding a purpose in employing those talents and abilities. Just like Slacker and the athlete, if you are driven by selfish desires, any accomplishment will seem shallow and unsatisfying. But if you have a noble purpose behind your drive, suddenly life becomes much more satisfying.

A well-defined purpose will drive all of your decisions and all of your actions. Finding your purpose will give your life direction and an achievement above your selfish-desires. Your finances are not your money; your finances are the choices you make, the priorities you set, and the planning you do about money. If your purpose will guide your decisions, choices, and actions, then a strong purpose will also guide your finances.

Money, Money, Money...Money

"What do you want to do when you grow up," a father asks his son.

"I want to make money," the son replies. "Lots and lots of money."

The father smiles at the response. A few years earlier, he wanted to be a doctor. Before that his childlike dream was to be a fireman. The father smiles again, this time uncomfortably, as he wonders how his son went from wanting to help people to wanting money.

"Have you checked the help-wanted?" the father asks. "Is there such a job as 'making money?'"

"Well, no, there is no such job, I guess," the son replies, "but you know what I mean. I want a job that pays well."

"Son, the people in life that just want money seem to never have any. Most successful people have found a way to help others or to give them something they want."

"What about drug dealers," the son says, "they are rich and they don't help people."

"That is my point son. This is an example of just making money. There are many ways to accumulate riches. I hope you find a way to be successful by helping people. It's more sustainable and a better life."

"I know, Dad, but I don't really know what I want to do. Why don't you pick a career for me?"

"I can't do that," the father smiles. "You have to find what you are passionate about. You need to discover your talents. You need to find what abilities you have and how to cultivate those abilities."

"How do I do that?" the son asks.

"Find ways to help people. As you do this, you will find something you are passionate about. After that, you will evaluate your abilities and the skills you need. Whether it is a job, a business, or a ministry, the money will follow. If you are genuinely helping people, the money will come."

It is sad to say, but many people will wander through an entire life without finding their purpose. They get so involved with the unimportant stuff that they just do what they must. No passion. No significance. No purpose. This is a shallow existence, but there is a better way.

Purpose

Why am I here? What is the meaning of life? Is there more to life than this? Generations of humans have asked these timeless questions. Is there any significance to my life beyond the daily grind? Is life really just a job I hate, making enough to barely scrape by, and very little beyond that? What happened to my dreams? When did life get so complicated that I stopped helping people? Why is there never enough money?

You will answer all of these questions in finding your purpose. The questions are basic meaning of life questions. Without a further exploration into the theological or spiritual aspects of the meaning of life, purpose gives you direction and a legacy of significance beyond yourself. Your purpose is the impression you make on the world. Your purpose is the action that influences the circumstances around you.

Finding your purpose is a process of self-discovery. The authors of this book have no expectation that your purpose will be revealed as you read the next few pages; however, in reading this, you can begin this process of self-discovery.

To discover your purpose, you must thoroughly answer three questions: 1) Who am I? 2) Who am I to be? and 3) Who or what am I to serve? The answers to these questions may be difficult to faithfully explore.

Who am I?

This question is the most introspective and possibly the most difficult to answer. In answering this question, you will recognize traits and habits in yourself that you like and others that you don't. You should ask this question from your own perspective, but also ask from the perspective of those closest to you. If you were your best friend, would you like you? If you were your spouse, child, or parent, would you be satisfied with how you fulfill your responsibilities? If you were your boss, would you be satisfied with the job you do? Ask these questions only of the people who somehow rely upon you. Do you make any difference in their lives? Can you look outside of yourself and see need in others' lives?

If you have peace with the answers to this first question, you may have already discovered your purpose, or at the very least, you are on the road to discovering your purpose. If you have found your purpose, there may be turmoil in your life, but you will meet that turmoil with a contentment and persistence to overcome and to fulfill your purpose. If this doesn't describe you, there is a contentment that can be attained when your life has direction and significance.

Who am I to Be?

Question number two is a forward looking question. If you already know the answer, then you probably know what your purpose is. With an unlimited range of career and service options, choosing one may seem daunting. In a perfect world, your purpose would just fall from the sky on the precise day you need it. Or, your purpose could be found in the riddle of a fortune cookie. Some people yearn fondly for the days when parents or a government official would choose their occupations. But your purpose is a special secret that only those diligent enough to seek out deserve to fulfill.

In the real world, the answer of "Who am I to be?" can be narrowed down based on your personality, your gifts, and your passion.

<u>Personality</u>. The first way to narrow your purpose is to identify your personality type. Taking a Jung Meyers-Briggs personality test or a similar personality test will reveal your true personality. The typical personality test categorizes your personality and generates a list of your strengths. From that list, the test generates a second list of professions that people with your personality currently fill. The professions list is typically expansive and will need to be further narrowed. A personality test is really just a snapshot that over time will reveal a true picture.

If you already have a type of work that excites your passion, then a personality test should affirm what you already know to be true. An interest in a particular field may reveal more about your personality than a test. Matching your personality to a range of alternatives will narrow your search for purpose.

Gifts. Everyone has talent. Some talents are more fashionable than others. If your talent is singing or athletic, you have a greater chance of being on television than if you have talent as a plumber. But if we were all talented singers and athletes, then our toilets wouldn't flush. You excel at something. Everyone has his or her own particular genius, or talent that just comes naturally.

Your abilities are another gift. Abilities are simply talents you have developed. The most talented musician can't find middle-C on a piano unless their talent is developed into ability. Your abilities take shape as you refine and develop your talents into something valuable to others.

Your list of career and service options is further narrowed by assessing your skills. Skills can be taught. The skills that you have learned may be the basis for your purpose. Because skills can be taught though, don't exclude any options based on a lack of skills. Just understand the skills you must develop to fulfill that purpose.

Passion. The most important component of identifying "Who am I to be?" is your passion. From the list of remaining alternatives, what purpose are you most passionate about pursuing? What do you live to do? What makes you wake up before your alarm in the morning and work all day long?

Many people have passive passions. Some people's passion is watching television. Some are passionate about watching sports. Others are passionate about sitting in church every Sunday. Your purpose will require a more active form of passion. "Who am I to be?" implies action. To live with purpose, you must develop an active passion. An active passion better utilizes your talents, abilities, and skills.

Who or What am I to Serve?

Do you serve your money? That may be a silly question, but consider it seriously. Does your money serve you, or do you serve your money? Your spending will answer this question. Do you live in a house that matches your family needs, or do you live in a house as big as you can afford? Do you drive the car you need, or do you drive the fanciest car you can afford? Do you spend just what you need, or do you spend everything you have? Are you trapped in your job because another job would alter your lifestyle? Do you work ridiculous hours and spend no time with your family because of the financial obligation you have? Do you live independently of your finances or do you live the life you can afford? Do you serve your money?

The first two questions about self-discovery determine what you are capable of doing. Determining who or what you are to serve helps you answer the "why" questions of life. Discovering purpose is more about "who" or "what" we serve than merely how we serve.

Serving money, or your own selfish interest, is very shallow and unfulfilling. When your purpose is strictly selfish, you will still question if there is more to life. Humans are designed to pursue a greater purpose, especially when all of our basic needs are met.

A life that leaves a legacy is one that serves others. Serving others is a very fulfilling purpose. Servanthood in every aspect of your life gives you a natural life with meaning. Service to others is foundational to a purpose with significance.

Purpose is a process of self-discovery. This begins by asking the three questions: 1) Who am I? 2) Who am I to be? and 3) Who or what am I to serve? These questions will help you discern how your talents, abilities, skills, and passion can be employed in the service of others. How do you know if you have found your purpose? Some believe that finding your purpose will eliminate all contention, but discovering a purpose will not eliminate hardship and turmoil from your life. Many people without purposeful lives are very comfortable. Following your purpose may unleash obstacles and challenges you would never see in the comfort of your monotony. The key to purpose is how you handle these tumultuous situations. When troubles come, focusing on your purpose gives you a peace and contentment that these obstacles can be overcome. Purpose will simplify your life. Instead of wondering why you work everyday, your purpose will guide these daily actions. Remember, though, discovery of purpose is only the first step.

Goals

Your purpose will drive everything else in your planning. Are you sure your purpose is right for you? This is how we find out. In this next step, set at least one goal in fulfilling your purpose. These goals must be specific, must be somehow measurable, must have a deadline, and must be written down.

Specific. Your goals are more attainable if they are specific. With this step, give your goal a title. For instance, if you want to be a doctor, "Doctor" is your title. If you feel called to the mission field, "Guatemala Mission" is your title. If you want to start a small business, give your company a working name. At this stage, don't worry about the specifics of attaining your goal; you will do that later. Right now just give it a name.

Measurable. Your goals must be concrete. "I want to be a better person." "I want to be healthier." These are wishes and not goals. Your goals must be measurable. Measurable doesn't necessarily mean it must be measured in inches, pounds, or even dollars. But you must determine tangibly if you achieved your goal or not. Examples of this are a medical degree or the opening of a small business. Making a goal measurable increases its specificity. The more specific the goal, the better your plan will be. Your measurable goal should not be a dollar amount. A dollar amount of money is a shallow goal. Money to complete a goal is a valid objective, or means to achieve a goal. Remember what money is and what it is not. Money is just a tool or a unit of measure.

Deadline. Every goal should have a completion date. Procrastination is the natural enemy of every goal. Without a deadline, you can defer action indefinitely on your goal. A passed deadline is not a reason to give up on a goal, but the deadline forces you to focus on action. A deadline is a recognition of patience that may be needed, and procrastination that must be avoided.

Written. Habakkuk 2:2 says, *"Write the vision and make it plain on tablets, That he may run who reads it."* (NKJV) Your goal will evolve or even change. At this point, it is important to make your goals concrete by writing them down. Writing your goals gives them a life that they would never have if they simply stay inside your crowded brain. This step also includes telling others about your goal. You shouldn't buy a billboard to advertise your goals to the world, just tell those closest to you and those who are affected by your decisions. Both positive and negative comments help in analyzing your goals.

Analysis

In analyzing your goals, you must determine both why you can achieve your goals, and reasons you cannot achieve your goals. What talents and abilities do you have or do you lack? What resources do you have at your disposal, and what resources must you acquire? Your analysis must be honest and must look at both the positive and the negative in achieving your goals. First, look at your strengths and opportunities. Next evaluate your weaknesses and threats.

<u>Strengths and Opportunities</u>. Your strengths are the skills, talents, abilities and resources you have that will help you succeed at your goal. Listing your strengths will encourage you that the goal you set is attainable because these strengths are at your disposal.

Opportunities will be open to you in the future and will help you achieve your goal. For instance, if someone sets a goal to graduate from college, an opportunity may be a scholarship that you qualify for. To be classified as an opportunity, it must be probable that it will be there. Winning the lottery is not an opportunity, it is a delusion. This list of strengths and opportunities is important encouragement. This list is the proof to you that your goal is within reach. The items on this list can be drawn upon to achieve your goal.

<u>Weaknesses and Threats</u>. Weaknesses are the skills, talents, abilities, and resources you lack to accomplish your goal. This list is not meant to discourage you. These are the attributes you lack that must be developed or overcome to attain your goal. A weakness may be a skill that must be developed, education that you need, or $20,000 to get started. Some weaknesses may be easily

overcome; others may take some creativity and determination to conquer.

Threats are obstacles that you will conceivably face in the future. These are roadblocks standing in the way of achieving your goal. The list of threats is limitless: locust, plague, pestilence, hail, fire, and brimstone. You can't prepare for every threat, but focus on the most likely threats. If you need a certain certification to complete your goal, then failure to complete that certification could be listed as a threat. Other threats may come from external sources such as a downturn in the economy, or a change in family situation. With a list of threats, you can think about some contingencies to overcome these threats. Inevitably, a threat will develop that is not part of your plan. This is where a plan must be flexible and you must persistently pursue your goal.

Objectives

Your objectives are the specific steps you must complete to achieve your goal. An ambitious goal will have several steps to achievement. Each of these steps is an objective.

Each objective will be a point on a roadmap to reaching your goal. For instance, if your goal is to become an electrician, your list of objectives may be: 1) earn $7,000 for electricians' school, 2) graduate and become certified, 3) complete an apprenticeship, 4) send out resumes and get hired. This is perhaps an over simplification, but these are the four general steps to achieving the goal of becoming an electrician. The more detailed your list of objectives are, the better your plan will be. Each objective should have a date attached with it to keep you on track to achieve your goal by its completion date.

Defining your objectives simply gives you a roadmap to follow in reaching your goal. In defining your objectives, you list the steps necessary to fulfill your goals. You can set your objectives up chronologically or by priority. Take note of any objective that must be met before you can move on to the next one. Some objectives may be worked on concurrently.

With most goals, at least one objective will be a sum of money. Most goals cost some amount of money to fulfill. The objective of saving an amount of money is your financial objective and Chapter 8 delves into the intricacies of saving for a financial objective.

Action

Action is the most difficult, but most important step. With the action step, you give life to your plan. Anyone can determine their purpose. Setting goals to fulfill that purpose is easy. Setting a series of objectives based on careful analysis is simple. But action is truly the only means of finding significance. Your greatest dream, your best goal, your most thought out plan is nothing without action.

To be successful, your action must have several attributes. Your action must be persistent, flexible, and focused. All three of these characteristics of action are important to achieving your goal and fulfilling your purpose.

First, persistent action is necessary to achieving your goal. Despite a careful evaluation of threats to your goal, something will come up that could derail your plan. A threat you anticipate may be more severe; or a threat you can't anticipate may stand in your way. If your goal truly fulfills your purpose, then your action must be persistent to overcome. Persistence may also be required in the everyday monotony of acting toward your goal. You may be a person that thrives when your goal is threatened; but you must also roll up your sleeves and do the everyday work to accomplish your goal.

Flexibility in your action is also necessary to achieve your goal. Despite your best planning efforts, you will face the unexpected in pursuing your goal. A failure, or even an unexpected success, may force you to change your plan. As the reality of your circumstance changes, your plan must also change to reflect this new reality. Flexibility should not conflict with your persistence. Flexibility shouldn't be an excuse to take shortcuts; but should be used to overcome threats and take advantage of new opportunities.

The final attribute of action is focus. In your actions, you should maintain a focus on your purpose. Focusing on your purpose will give your persistence an incentive. Focusing on your purpose will guide your flexibility. Flexibility can include shortcuts around your purpose, and opportunities that may take you away from your purpose. Focusing on your purpose will help you choose when to be flexible and when to be persistent.

Focusing on your purpose will guide your decisions. Consider a doctor whose purpose is reconstructive surgery for burn victims in a region with a low standard of living. The doctor gets a job offer that pays $75,000 more to perform plastic surgery in a much more affluent area. Should this doctor take advantage of this opportunity? How does this fulfill her purpose? Will she perform her duties with the same passion and reward? Focus on purpose will help this doctor accept or decline this opportunity.

Action toward a purpose-filled goal is best accomplished with persistence, flexibility, and focus on your purpose. When your actions are planned through objectives, based on fully analyzed goals that fulfill your purpose, then the action will be very natural. Instead of waking up every morning wondering why you hate your job, you have a document explaining your actions. You will know what you plan to accomplish. You will know specifically how you will meet goals, and it is all based on your passion and ability.

Jane the Student, for Example

Jane is a twenty year old college student. She has just completed her sophomore year as an accounting major. She has good grades in her general studies courses, but in her accounting classes, she has done poorly and has really lost interest in accounting. She struggles with the decision to change her major. In addition, about six months ago, she received a second-degree burn on her hand when she touched her hot plate. Her injury is healing, but she constantly thinks about the children she saw at the burn center with serious physical and emotional scars. She wants to help.

Jane's Purpose

To discover her purpose, Jane begins with the three questions of self-discovery: 1) Who am I? 2) Who am I to be? and 3) Who am I to serve? In answering "Who am I?" Jane realizes her unhappiness with accounting. She has no interest, much less passion, for it. Her high school counselor said it was a good profession, but it just isn't for her.

The next question, "Who am I to be?" is more difficult to answer, but she must answer it, as it is not good enough to just know what she doesn't want to be. Jane is genuinely interested in health care, and decides this reveals more about her personality than a test. Jane is a gifted student. She does well in her science classes, and her GPA is strong except for two D's in accounting. Jane is passionate about helping children like the ones at the burn center. While she has some friends who switch majors with every new life experience, Jane is certain this life experience left an unforgettable impression on her.

In answering "Who am I to serve?" Jane is very introspective. She isn't changing majors for her parents. Both her parents are very happy with accounting. Money factors into her decision, but she dwells more on the money she must spend up front for medical school than the money she would make as a doctor. Jane is determined to serve others through healing. Jane writes down her purpose as:

To serve others by healing burn victims

The Goal

Jane sets her goal. She wants to become a doctor who specializes in reconstructive surgery. Jane gives her goal the general title of "Doctor." She does some research and determines she will measurably be a doctor when she passes the state board exam. She gives her goal a seven-year deadline. She writes all of this down:

Doctor
Pass the state board seven years from today

Jane tells her friends and family. Her mother and brother are happy for her and tell her she has the temperament and personality to be a good doctor. Her friends tell her most of her grades are good enough to get into medical school except the D's she has in two accounting classes. Her father lovingly smiles and warns of a big commitment in both time and money. She must do it mostly on her own because he can't afford to help financially. Jane will use this information in her analysis.

The Analysis

Jane's analysis begins with the strengths and weaknesses she has in becoming a doctor. She lists the following strengths:

Good student
Two years of scholarship at the university
An aptitude for science
Well paying summer job

Next, she lists the following opportunities:
Health care is a growing industry
Availability of loans and scholarships
A program to pay off student loans by practicing in a rural area

After analyzing the positives, Jane looks to her weaknesses and threats. Jane lists the weaknesses she must overcome to reach her goal:

Inadequate GPA from the D's in accounting
No money for medical school

The threats are assessed next:
Grades are not good enough
Can't get into medical school
Can't complete medical school while accumulating student loan debt

The Objectives

Jane reviews her purpose and goal and reevaluates her analysis. Now she generates her objectives. Her GPA is adequate but the two D's in accounting is a problem. Jane writes her first objective:

> *1. Retake the two accounting classes to achieve a B or better*

Here is an important point about finding your purpose. Once you discover your purpose, your life doesn't automatically reset. You may have a mess to clean up first. Cleaning up that mess is the first objective in fulfilling your purpose. Jane has a mess, but it is small. Finding your purpose will not allow you to escape your life. Take care of your mess before you continue. Your mess may be bigger. Whether your mess is a big pile of debt, or an addiction to which you turned, clean it up. Your mess may be a result of your own mistakes, or circumstances beyond your control, but you need to clean the slate and take care of your mess.

From there, Jane lists the next series of objectives:

> 2. *Get a part time job and save $25,000 (immediately and in 2 years)*
> 3. *Graduate with a 3.85 GPA (2 years)*
> 4. *Be accepted to medical school (2 years)*
> 5. *Graduate medical school (6 years)*
> 6. *Pass the state boards (7 years)*

At this point, the objectives are vague, especially the more distant objectives. Objective number two is a financial objective that must be met to complete the remaining objectives. As time passes and you act on your plan, you must further refine and specify your objectives. This must be a living document that changes as circumstances change.

Action

Jane starts immediately. She goes to the registrar and changes her major to pre-med. She enrolls in the two accounting classes and makes an appointment to meet with an advisor in the biology department. She picks up a newspaper to check out the help wanted section. With a renewed vigor, Jane returns to her studies, knowing exactly where she is headed. Whenever she doubts, or faces obstacles, she has a document to remind her of her purpose, her goals, and the objectives or steps to completing her goals.

The first step in setting any goal is discerning some purpose in the accomplishment. If your goal is to become a millionaire, you will find that this very attainable goal is just a number. If you set a goal of financial security, you will find there is very little security derived from your finances. In setting your goal, it is important to find a purpose greater than yourself. Once you determine that purpose, then setting goals is simple. And with the goal, you will ultimately create a plan with specific objectives to fulfill that goal.

On a Rock: Your Purpose

Finding your purpose has significance beyond your finances. A well-defined purpose in your life will guide all of your actions including your financial decisions. As a financial principle, your purpose will guide your income, your choices, your giving, your spending, and will be the basis for your savings. A well-defined purpose will orchestrate every part of your financial life.

Your purpose will affect every aspect of your financial life. Your purpose impacts your income in two ways. First, you can fulfill your purpose through your work. Second, your earnings can be used to indirectly fulfill your purpose.

Your purpose will greatly influence your choices. If spending on your purpose is your greatest want, you can structure your choices to minimize your spending on needs and focus your wants on fulfilling your purpose. You will make every decision and choices mindful of your purpose. With purposeful choices, you will structure your financial life to spend for value, give from your abundance, and save to fulfill your purpose.

Knowing your purpose will clarify ways to express your servant's heart. You already give in recognition of your abundance and to demonstrate your prioritized values. With a well-defined purpose, charitable giving is no longer a necessary inconvenience. It is a direct fulfillment of your purpose. With a servant's heart, giving is only the start; you will also seek new ways to fill needs in others.

Perhaps the greatest impact of discovering your purpose is in your planned spending. With a purposeless life, you will spend your money in an attempt to fill a mysterious void. Every human will strive for significance. If you have no purpose, you will spend money on things to achieve significance. But this spending will only create a larger void that even more spending will never fill.

With a well-defined purpose, every dollar you earn already has a reason to be spent, saved, or given. You will spend money to fulfill your purpose and your life will have meaning. Instead of a storage shed full of meaningless treasures, you will have a legacy of truly helping others.

Your purpose also necessitates saving and provides the impetus for saving. Instead of saving for all of the things others tell you to save for, you will save for your distinct purpose. Saving will not be a burden, as your growing finances will be targeted to something specific. Large piles of money have very little significance; saving to fulfill your purpose will have a legacy of fulfillment.

Every component of your financial foundation works together. Your income determines the level of your choices. The consumer choices you make will determine the amount you give, spend, and save. With charitable giving, you will recognize your abundance and prioritize your values. Your prioritized values are carefully considered in a written spending plan. The spending plan must be faithfully executed in a noisy marketplace. Finally, your savings will complete the buffer in your financial life. All of these actions will be taken to fulfill your purpose. When this happens, your financial foundation works in concert toward the fulfillment of your purpose. Your money no longer controls your life, your purpose guides and directs your life. Your money is simply a tool driving your purpose.

Chapter 8 looks at the final piece of your solid financial foundation. Savings is an important final building block for your financial foundation. Saving for a purpose is how you will build on that foundation.

Your solid financial foundation:

- Income
- Choice
- Charitable Giving
- Planned Spending
- Savings
- Held together with the mortar of Purpose

8 Your Savings

Most children have a piggy bank, and these little money holders come in all shapes and sizes. From the plain Mason jar to the ceramic pig-shaped bank, they all have the same purpose: saving our treasured coins. Do you remember your piggy bank? Do you remember how you used it? The objects we wanted were far beyond our meager income. Two dollars per week doesn't go very far for an eight-year-old. However, if we deposited our coins in our piggy bank, eventually we could buy whatever we wanted. The concept of saving was so simple.

As adults, we are much more sophisticated. Instead of this childish waiting-for-our-money-to-grow, we now buy with credit and pay it back later. Most creditors even spread the payment over a series of months so the lump sum doesn't shock our sensibilities. But here's a question for you: do you enjoy the sophistication of debt, or do you long for the simpler times of childlike savings?

So many people have bought into the debt lie that savings is becoming an outdated concept. Have you ever saved and paid cash for a car? Managers and finance departments scurry to complete this "strange" transaction. As strange as it may seem, you pay less money on a real basis using cash from savings than if you pay with debt. If saving is more advantageous, then why is it so difficult? The answer is simple. When you were a child, usually you only saved when you had a tangible reason; you saved for something specific. And the same applies to your life now; you must tie a savings objective to a goal derived from your purpose.

The Bible Told Me So

Whether you believe the Bible is the divinely inspired Word of God, or just a collection of fables, interesting proverbs, and clear moral code, it contains many valuable financial truths. One of the more interesting stories is of a young Hebrew boy named Joseph. In the short version of his life story, his jealous brothers sell him into slavery in Egypt where his diligent labor lands him in jail. After being forgotten for 13 years, he is promoted from the basement prison to CEO of Egypt, inc. simply by interpreting one of the Pharaoh's dreams. The dream indicates seven years of plenty followed by seven years of famine. So, before Joseph gets settled into his corner office with a view of the pyramids, he knows of the impending famine.

Here we will pick up the story. Joseph enacts a simple plan: for the seven years of plenty, they store one-fifth, or twenty percent, of their harvest. They put this harvest in a storehouse. Again, that is one-fifth of all their harvest, and in more modern terms, they saved twenty percent of their income during the good times.

After the seven plentiful years, the famine comes just as Joseph predicts. So what happens to Egypt? Do they barely survive? To the contrary, they prosper. They not only sustain their own people, but also sell surplus to neighboring countries, and Egypt becomes the dominant force in the region.

So how does this story from antiquity apply to us? You don't have strange dreams, and even if you did, you don't know a Joseph to interpret them. Can these concepts actually work in our own lives? The answer is a resounding "Yes!" First, while we may not know the exact timing, sustenance, abundance and famine can all be easily identified in our financial lives. Sustenance is when you monetarily meet your family's basic need for food, shelter, and clothing. Abundance is any income above and beyond these basic items. Financial famines are also easily identified. When your income drops below your sustenance level, you are in a famine. This may happen if you lose your job, suffer a disability, or any number of circumstances. For some of us, the famines we face are self-imposed like: retirement, changing jobs, or starting a small business. While these are great opportunities and must be entered with careful planning, these transitions cause at least a partial financial famine. All of us will have periods in our lives of both abundance and famine; what determines our success is how we have used the times of abundance to plan for our famines.

In the story of Joseph, we can see a tremendous strategy of how to navigate through the ups and downs of income. He commanded all of Egypt to store one-fifth of everything made during the seven years of plenty. They saved twenty percent of their income, and notice that they didn't save twenty percent of the leftovers after everyone was full. They saved twenty percent of the *total*. Similarly, when we are in a time of abundance, we should save twenty percent of our income. The result for Egypt was prosperity in time of famine, and with healthy savings, we will reap a similar prosperity in our times of financial famine.

First Things First

A child sneaks out the front door of her house with her brother's oversized bicycle helmet strapped to her head. She creeps to the oversized bicycle and climbs on the seat. She pushes the pedal with the handle bars swiveling wildly. Before the child can push the second pedal, the bicycle topples and crashes to the concrete driveway.

A parent hears the commotion and runs out the door. A crying child melts into her mother's arms as she assesses the situation.

"I just wanted to ride a bike," the child sobs into her mothers shoulder.

"I wish you had told me," the mother replies, "we have a smaller bike with training wheels."

"Training wheels?" the child asks.

"Yes…they keep the bike stable so you can learn all of the motions. Training wheels are the easiest way to learn to ride a bike."

Saving money can be complicated! You can put your money in a number of places. Your money can go in a bank checking account, savings account, or certificate of deposit. You can store your money in a retirement account or brokerage account. You can spend your money in a life insurance policy with a cash reserve. All of these options are offered by hundreds of firms with dozens of products to choose from. And then there's always the option of hiding your money in a sock under your bed.

Let's start with training wheels. The "training wheels" for savings is an emergency fund. To be clear on its purpose, we call ours a "storehouse fund," similar to Joseph's. A storehouse fund has several factors.

First, your money must be accessible without penalty, so this means you must have a checking or savings account.

Your first goal is to include at least three to six months of living expenses in your storehouse fund. Remember, your monthly living expense is calculated by your monthly gross income minus taxes, savings, charitable giving, and any luxuries you will eliminate in a crisis. Your storehouse fund must be greater than all of your monthly obligations like mortgage payments, tax bill, car payments, and any other monthly payments. In addition, the number of months you need saved will be determined by your lifestyle. If your job is secure in a stable industry, you have very few health issues, and no risky hobbies, then three months may be adequate; however, for most people, six months is probably the appropriate amount. If your cash flow is seasonal, your storehouse fund may swell to nine months or a year to accommodate your lack of income. And then, as you approach retirement, or a time when you will rely on your savings, your storehouse fund should be maintained at two years living expenses.

The amount in your storehouse fund is expressed in the following equation:

Storehouse Fund = (monthly Income – monthly taxes, saving, and giving) × number of months

Finally, your storehouse fund is only used in times of financial famine or real need. If abundance is any income above basic needs, then famine is when your income cannot cover those basic needs. Be very aware that as your storehouse fund grows, you will be tempted to spend it. The list of spending temptation includes but is not limited to: investment opportunities, monthly expenses, consumer goods, a vacation, holiday spending, fixing your car, house, dishwasher, and the list goes on and on. And just to note: a big screen TV the Friday before the big game is *not* an emergency. It is very important to guard your storehouse fund. Without this fund, you have very few options in a crisis, and none of those options are good.

Your Storehouse Fund

Your storehouse fund is built in three easy steps: 1) Beginning, 2) Building, and 3) Maintenance. During the beginning phase, you will direct at least twenty percent of your monthly income into this fund. This is good practice in structuring your life to achieve this twenty percent figure. All savings and investments go toward your storehouse fund until you pass the beginning stage. Any unexpected inflow of cash like a tax refund or a bonus at work should be applied to the storehouse fund. In this phase, understand the value of your fund and focus every extra dollar into the fund. If you are serious about your storehouse fund, you may even consider selling some of your junk to boost your fund.

In the building stage, twenty percent of your income is placed into the designated account until you have three months of living expenses. The building stage can continue until you have six months of living expenses. Again, the number of months is based on the stability of your employment, your health and lifestyle, and the availability of any other long-term investments. The building stage continues until you reach your target number for your storehouse fund.

The maintenance stage is the easiest…just keep your paws off of it! Only in cases of financial famine should you dip into this fund. In addition, you will need to periodically increase your storehouse fund to reflect any changes in your monthly spending. In this maintenance stage you must replenish any funds used during an emergency.

Foolproof Investment Scheme

A man has a dream. He wants enough money to quit his job and travel around the country in a motor home. It seems like a big goal, but this man has a dream and a foolproof investment scheme. His plan is very simple. Every Wednesday and Saturday afternoon, this man buys twenty dollars of Super Jackpot Lottery tickets. Every Wednesday and Saturday night he perches in front of his television and watches the drawing. His eyes are fixed on his twenty tickets as the dancing balls jump from the machine and the numbers line up on the screen. Usually one or two numbers match his tickets. Sometimes he gets three or four numbers to match. Once he even got five matching numbers; but this lottery requires six matching numbers to win the millions of dollars. After the drawing, this man drops his tickets into his wastebasket. He isn't frustrated though, because next Wednesday he will take his twenty dollars to the convenience store and purchase twenty tickets more. This man has a dream and a plan.

A woman has a dream. She wants a beach house for her retirement. She dreams of no financial cares; just quiet walks on the beach. It may seem like a big goal, but this woman has a dream and a foolproof investment scheme. This woman has a son who has a beautiful singing voice. His mother has pushed him for years to become the next teen singing sensation. Once he becomes a pop star, he will be rich and famous and will buy his beloved mother that dreamy beach house; or so she thinks. It can be expensive. With the thousands of dollars spent on singing lessons, agent tryouts, and specialized training, it is a financial drain. Granted, it would be helpful if her son would enjoy it more and be more passionate about his singing but other than that, her plan for the beach house is foolproof.

Both of these examples may seem foolish to you. After all, when we do the math, if this man took that $40 per week and instead invested in the stock market, historically it could return about $2 million dollars over a forty-year working life ($40 per week for forty years, 12% annual return and the $2 million is before the effects of inflation are accounted for). And the woman could just save the thousands of dollars per year and stop hassling her son. You may scoff and maybe even chuckle at the folly of each plan. But they might have one up on you: at least they *have* a plan. Is your savings plan any better? Do you even have one?

Saving

At this point, you need a financial objective based on a goal that fulfills your purpose. If part of your purpose is taking care of your family, you may set a goal of owning your own home. Your financial objective may be $30,000 for a down payment. Or, if your purpose requires a goal of graduating from college, your financial objective may be $20,000 to help offset the cost of tuition. Your financial objective will help you achieve a goal that fulfills your purpose.

Creating a savings plan to reach a financial objective involves five factors:

1. Estimate your current savings
2. Place a dollar amount on your objective
3. Establish a time frame
4. Prioritize your savings
5. Determine your monthly contribution

You must systematically follow these steps to create a savings plan.

Because you already have a financial objective, the remaining steps easily fall into place. A difficult factor in saving is determining why to save; however, if you know your purpose, your goals, and the objectives, saving is now more purposeful.

Step one: Estimate your current savings

This step seems obvious, but is often overlooked. Categorizing your savings is actually more important than knowing how much you have saved. What portion of your savings is devoted to your storehouse fund? Should you build a storehouse fund first? Are you saving for a financial objective? Do you have savings not yet targeted to a specific financial objective? Answering these questions will help you determine your starting point.

Step two: Place a dollar value on your objective

"How much does a degree in accounting cost?" the voice on the telephone asks.

The clerk at the university registrar's office contemplates this question for a moment and responds, "This year's tuition and fees are…"

"No, no, no. I need the total cost for the full four years. I'm saving for college three years from now. I need to know how much money I need to get a degree in accounting."

"The total cost is difficult to estimate for this year. It will depend on how many credits you take, how much your textbooks cost, your living expenses, and any incidental costs. That cost is multiplied over four or five years, and the costs will continue to go up every year."

"So how much should I save?" the voice on the phone again asks.

"I'm not a fortune teller," the clerk replies. She waits a moment for a laugh that doesn't come and continues, "There are several references that can give you an average cost of college. There are also scholarships and financial aid available to most students. If I were you, I would save all that you can for the next three years. It probably won't be enough, but it will help you with your goal of completing an accounting degree."

"Huh…Save all that I can. I'll sure try that. Thank you."

The second step estimates the amount of money you will save for your financial objective. For many people, this is the most difficult step. Most savings goals involve spending in the future. Because of this, there are many variables in accurately predicting that future cost. Regardless of your financial objective, inflation will diminish the purchasing power of your savings. Some things, like education, have actually gone up in cost faster than inflation. Advances in technology and innovation also drive up costs faster than inflation alone. As products and services become more advanced, they cost more on an inflation adjusted basis. These obstacles are not reasons to avoid saving, but they are considerations to make your savings plan more realistic.

Whatever your financial objective, research what amount is needed. In your research, you may find an average for a good starting point. Adjust that average to reflect your specific objective. This step is a roadblock for many savers. You may think, "If I can't pin-point the amount, then how do I complete the process, and how do I ever save?" To avoid this roadblock, create your best-guess number and move on to the next step. Know that your plan must adjust to reality as time progresses. Your number is not accurate, but is only a problem if you fail to adapt your plan.

Know that your estimate is the best you can do and proceed to the next step.

Step three: Establish a time frame

Spending, by its nature, occurs in the present. On the other hand, savings accumulate over time. Because of this, your plan must acknowledge the length of your savings period. This in turn determines your monthly savings.

Goals and financial objectives can have an inherent time frame. A fourteen year old who sets a goal of graduating from college has an inherent time frame of four to eight years; four years until he begins college and eight before he graduates. A forty-five year old has a goal of retiring at fifty-five to volunteer at a homeless shelter full time. The inherent time frame will be ten years to death. If you won't spend your savings in a lump sum, then you must note the time frame you will save and the time you will spend. If your goal has an inherent time frame, then step three is simple.

Most saving, however, is due to a lack of money today. You would buy your house tomorrow, but you don't have the funds available. You would open a small business tomorrow, but you don't have the lump sum of money to get started. In these situations, your time frame is the amount of money needed divided by the amount you can save per month.

Step four: Prioritize your savings

"*Dear Santa,*" the seven year old boy writes at the top of a lined page.

"*I have been a good boy this year,*" the boy writes carefully. "*My list is short. For Christmas, I want a BB gun, a football, a remote control car, a cowboy hat, a fire engine, a train set, a bicycle, and a pony. And no clothes."*

The little boy signs his name and adds this p.s., "*I have been really good this year.*"

Sometimes our list of financial objectives will look similar to this Christmas list. If you are ambitious and have a well defined purpose, you will save for more than you have money to save. This step helps you sort out which financial objectives are best to save for now, and which to save for later. So how do you prioritize your savings? Your first priority should be a storehouse fund. All twenty percent of your savings should be directed to your storehouse fund. After your storehouse fund, your savings can be targeted to one financial objective, or it can be split to fund several objectives.

There are several factors to consider. First, you should consider the amount. It is easier to achieve a financial objective with a small price tag instead of a large one. The second consideration is the time frame. If a financial objective must be met quickly, it may be a higher priority than a financial objective in the distant future. This may also include chronology. If one financial objective must be completed before you can move on to the next, then it must be a higher priority. Remember to view your priorities through the prism of your purpose.

Goals can either be self-sufficient or must be funded through external sources. A goal that provides income like a career or a small business is self sufficient. A goal that does not generate income like volunteer work, retirement, or a ministry must be funded through external sources. This is a consideration in your prioritizing. A financial objective that leads to self-sufficiency or even cash generating may be a higher priority. For instance, saving for college should be a higher priority than saving for retirement because with a college degree, your earnings will be higher and saving for retirement easier. Saving money to start a small business should be a priority because, if successful, the income from that small business can generate savings for other financial objectives that meet goals to fulfill your purpose.

As you prioritize, you shouldn't necessarily give up on a financial objective. You must determine what you will save for now, and what you will save for in the future. In saving twenty percent of your income, you will accumulate these savings quickly.

Step Five: Determine your monthly contribution

Step five is a difficult step, especially if you have several financial objectives you would like to fund. With the first four steps, you focus your savings on your purpose. Step five gives you the action plan based on this focus.

Step one describes the starting point. You only need to save above and beyond your accumulated savings. In step two, you understand how much you must save to fulfill your financial objective. Step three explains the duration, either an inherent time until it is needed, or the amount of time needed to accumulate funds. With step four you prioritize which financial objectives are the most to least important. With step five, you will determine how much of your savings will go to each financial objective and how you will save and invest that money. This is determined based on how much you currently have, how much you will need, when you will need it, and which objectives are most important.

Step five is approached from one of two different directions. You can save either 1) a disposable amount from your monthly budget, or 2) twenty percent of your before tax income. Both approaches are valid, and both should leave you a fixed monthly amount to apply to a financial objective.

With the first method, you determine how much money you have left after all of your expenses are met, after which your money is allocated based on priority. Your storehouse fund should be your first priority, and your savings should be directed there until you reach the maintenance stage. Then the remaining money should be allocated. If your first priority has an inherent time frame, you may not devote all of your savings to this category. The monthly contribution can be determined with the following equation:

Monthly contribution =
total needed ÷ the years until needed ÷ 12.

With a longer term saving objective, your total amount must factor inflation. If you are competent with a computer or a financial calculator, the variables of today's values, total pay period, and an estimated inflation rate can be imputted to determine the amount needed. Table 1 can also be used to determine the inflation factor.

Table 1: Inflation Factors*

3 years	1.12
5 years	1.22
10 years	1.48
15 years	1.80
20 years	2.19
30 years	3.24

*The inflation factor assumes 4% inflation

The following equation uses the inflation factor to determine an inflation adjusted monthly contribution:
Monthly contribution =

$$\text{total amount} \times \text{inflation factor} \div \text{years} \div 12$$

For example, if you are saving for a car that costs $24,000 that you want to buy three years from now, the monthly contribution would be:

Monthly contribution =

$$\$24{,}000 \times 1.12 \div 3 \div 12 = \$746.67$$

In saving this amount every month, in three years this person will have enough to purchase this car with cash.

If you choose the second method of saving twenty percent of your income, the process is very similar. The difference is that your twenty percent may be greater than the monthly contribution you determine. Because of this, you may fund several of your financial objectives at the same time. This again is based on your priority.

The primary difference between the two methods is the forced savings. Most people who save what is left after expenses often find there is very little left. We have a tendency to spend all of our money when we are not intentional about saving. Saving intentionally means setting aside a predetermined amount every month as savings. You may begin by saving ten or fifteen percent. There is no commandment saying you must save twenty percent. The Bible simply alludes that prosperous blessings are the result of purposeful savings. This blessing, again from our Biblical example, isn't in good times, but as a result of some challenge. A strong savings transforms most challenges into opportunities.

Building Your House

Let's take you, for example. Pretend your purpose includes caring for your family, and one of your goals is purchasing a new home. Based on this, you set a financial objective of $30,000 for a down payment. You will buy this home in three years. The other saving you need is to strengthen your storehouse fund. Let's assume your monthly income is $4,000. Saving twenty percent per month is $800. We will use the five step savings evaluation to determine our savings plan.

Step One: Estimate you current savings

Right now, you have $842 dollars in your checking account. Most of this will be spent before the end of the month. You also have $5,000 in a savings account for your storehouse fund. Based on your monthly income minus savings, taxes, and tithe of ten percent, your monthly need is $2,360. You want four months of living expenses, so your storehouse fund should be $9,440 ($2,360 × 4 months). You sigh and think about the saving time that will be wasted on building your storehouse fund, but caring for your family should include their security. At this point, your current savings is $5,000.

Step Two: Place a dollar value on your objective

The two savings objectives you focus on are $9,440 for a storehouse fund, and $30,000 for the down payment. Fortunately, you haven't picked a specific house; you just have a price range. The need for a storehouse fund is static right now, but can be adjusted upward as needed. You feel comfortable enough with the two numbers that you write them down and you move on to step three.

Step Three: Establish a time frame

You set a goal of purchasing a house in three years. You are skeptical if this is possible with your income, but you will try. Your storehouse fund has a less finite time frame. You should have a storehouse fund in place as soon as possible.

Step four: Prioritize your savings

Your savings plan is very simple. Your storehouse fund should always be your first priority. If your plan proceeds like you want, you could get your down payment, buy your house, get settled in, lose your job, and lose it all if you don't have the buffer of a storehouse fund. Your second priority will be the financial objective of $30,000 for your house.

Step Five: Determine your monthly contribution

We decide to save $800 per month. At this rate, the first six months will be devoted to your famine fund:

$$(\$9{,}440 - \$5{,}000) \div \$800 = 5.55 \text{ months}$$

After this, the calculation is more complicated. Your monthly contribution, as determined by the following equation is:

Monthly contribution =

$$\$30{,}000 \times 1.12 \div 3 \text{ years} \div 12 = \$933.33$$

Your heart leaps; but not in a good way. You can't catch your breath. Your monthly contribution is $133.33 greater than the twenty percent targeted to saving. You momentarily think about giving up.

Take a deep breath and calm down. Your goal is well within reach. Now comes the tough decisions. You can push back your time frame slightly. You also know that your pay will increase. Another very viable option is to devote a portion of your housing budget to savings. If you are currently renting, the amount you spend on mortgage payments, property taxes, homeowners insurance, maintenance and upkeep, and some utilities and public services will be higher. From a budgetary perspective, you can devote all of those potential costs to savings to prove over the next three years that your spending plan can handle that spending level on your housing. If the numbers don't add up, don't give up. This challenge requires some creativity and some stepping out in faith.

Do I Hide It in My Mattress?

A question that every saver asks is, "Where should I store my money?" The options are very difficult to sort through. You can put it in a checking account, savings account, money market account, money market fund, certificate of deposit, Treasury bills, Treasury notes, corporate bonds, municipal bonds, bond funds, stocks, mutual funds, index funds, derivatives, real estate funds or commodities; and this list is incomplete. For each category, there are thousands of securitites sold by hundreds of banks, brokers, and investment companies. Where do you start?

The intricacies of the potential savings vehicles is another book; however, here are some keys to getting started. Start saving with a bank savings account or a money market account or fund. These accounts have low minimums and there are few restrictions for withdrawing your money. The returns are low, but saving in these is very simple. You should keep your storehouse fund in this type of account. Be sure that your accounts are FDIC insured with a bank, NCUA insured with a credit union, or SIPC insured with a broker. If the bank becomes insolvent, you will get your money back up to $250,000 with this insurance. With your broker, the limit is $500,000.

If you save for one to five years, you will want something with a higher return. With this time frame, you will want something to offset the impact of inflation. Bank certificate of deposits (CDs) may be appropriate. A CD will require a greater minimum and you can't withdraw the money without paying a penalty. CDs are for specific time frames. To get the most out of your CDs, you should match your time frame, or remaining time frame, with the CD (1 year, 2 year, 3 year or 5 year). The returns on CDs are preset, but that preset rate changes, so shop around and find the best rate.

If your time frame is three to ten years, you want something to keep better pace with inflation and has the potential for tax advantage if you are in a higher tax bracket. For this three to ten year range, bonds or a bond fund is most appropriate. With funds greater than $50,000, you can buy a series of individual bonds, or for sums less than this you will want a bond mutual or index fund. Bond funds have a time frame attached with them also. The volatility of a bond fund can be measured by duration. The duration (2-20 years) is matched approximately to your time frame. If you are in a higher tax bracket, you will want the tax free advantage of municipal bonds instead of corporate bonds.

For investments from seven to ten years or greater, there are only a few investments that keep up with inflation after taxes. Equities or stocks are most appropriate for this time frame. Stocks and stock mutual or index funds are volatile. They go way up, and they go down. But in the long term, stocks historically outpace inflation after taxes. Mutual funds, and more specifically index funds, are the safest and simplest stock investment for your long term savings. These concepts, plus other things like IRAs, 401(k)s, and 529s, should be researched for the best place to store your money.

The complexity of investing is not an excuse to avoid saving. Saving your money in your mattress, is better than no savings at all. Saving intentionally to reach goals that fulfill your purpose is a great way for your money to serve you.

A Quick Word About Debt

Your credit score is not part of a solid financial foundation. Your home mortgage is not a building block of a solid financial foundation; neither is a credit card, a line of credit, or any consumer debt. A foundation of debt is a foundation built on sand. Proverbs 22:7 says, *"Just as the rich rule the poor, so the borrower is servant to the lender."* (NKJV) According to this proverb, the borrower and a lender have a servant and master relationship. Discovering your purpose asks the question, "Who am I to serve?" Do you serve your fellow man? Do you want to serve Christ? Or do you want to serve Master Card, Visa, and American Express?

If you are in debt, the twenty percent that would normally go to savings should be diverted to paying down your debt. If you have savings, your storms and challenges can become opportunities. If you are in debt, when you face storms and challenges, your turmoil amplifies.

If you are not in debt, be very judicious in how you use debt. You should never use debt for consumer goods or any asset that declines in value. You should never use debt to balance your monthly budget. You may need to use some debt to buy a house, but you should have at least a twenty percent down payment, and structure the payments for a fifteen year mortgage. You shouldn't be tied to your debt for thirty years. Any debt you acquire, whether for a car, a business, or for education, should have a serious down payment, and should be paid off quickly. You should be able to afford the item and should be able to fit the monthly payment in your spending plan. You will need a fully funded storehouse fund before you acquire any of this debt.

Avoid consumer debt at all costs. The fees, interest, and penalties make this debt very expensive. Again, the typical consumer will pay twelve to eighteen percent more with a credit card. You are prone to buy more than you can afford with debt. Find something better to serve than your lender.

On a Rock: Your Savings

Your ability to save is foundational to your finances. As you develop a spending plan, savings will force you to structure your spending plan with some margin for error. You will no longer live paycheck-to-paycheck if you have the buffer of savings. Saving for a strong storehouse fund will also smooth times of increased costs or decreased income. Your financial foundation is only as strong as your ability to maintain it. With a storehouse fund, you have the ability to shore up your foundation regardless of circumstance.

Your ability to save is foundational, but this is also the best way to grow your finances. Saving for a house, a car, a vacation or other major purchases helps you avoid debt and a financial house too heavy for its foundation. Saving for education, retirement, or money to open a small business will enhance your ability to fulfill your purpose. To be fruitful, all of your saving must be for a specific reason.

Tying your saving to your purpose gives you a meaningful reason to accumulate wealth. If you are just trying to build a pile of cash, your saving will be difficult and pointless. But if every dollar is targeted to accomplishing a specific goal, saving will be very natural and necessary. If you save for a financial objective, the reason for saving is evident and the remaining savings steps are simply about getting the math approximately right. The steps for saving and the equations you will need are found in the appendix at the end of the book.

Every component of your financial foundation works together. Your income determines the level of your choices. The consumer choices you make will determine the amount you give, spend, and save. With charitable giving, you will recognize your abundance and prioritize your values. Your prioritized values are carefully considered in a written spending plan. The spending plan must be faithfully executed in a noisy marketplace. Your storehouse fund will complete the buffer in your financial life. Your ability to save above and beyond a storehouse fund is the best means to grow a financial house upon this solid financial foundation. All of these actions will be taken to fulfill your purpose. When this happens, your financial foundation works in concert toward the fulfillment of your purpose. Your money no longer controls your life, your purpose guides and directs your life. Your money is simply a tool driving your purpose.

Chapter 9 puts all of the building blocks together. Chapter 9 will show you how a strong financial foundation will stand up to the storms of life. There is very little you can do to stop the financial storms from coming, but you *can* prepare your foundation to withstand these storms.

Your solid financial foundation:

- Income
- Choice
- Charitable Giving
- Planned Spending
- Savings
- Held together with the mortar of Purpose

9

ON A ROCK

YOUR SOLID FINANCIAL FOUNDATION

"Therefore whoever hears these sayings of Mine, and does them, I will liken him to a wise man who built his house on the rock: and the rains descended, the floods came, and the winds blew and beat on that house; and it did not fall, for it was founded on the rock. But everyone who hears these sayings of Mine and does not do them, will be like a foolish man who built his house on the sand: and the rain descended, the floods came, and the winds blew and beat on that house; and it fell, and great was its fall."

Matthew 7:24-27 (NKJV)

This bit of wisdom is specifically about your spiritual foundation. If you have a strong foundation, when the storms of life come, your spiritual house will stand. This book explains the relationship you have with your money. Money is just a representation of your work, your worth, and how you allocate your resources. From this perspective, the principle of building a strong foundation applies to your finances. Fulfilling your purpose in life is often contingent upon how strong your financial foundation is.

On Sand

Bill and Susie are average people. They both work hard and earn about $50,000 per year. Bill and Susie have two kids that they love, and a cat and a dog. They own their home and have two cars. They live comfortably, but not lavishly.

Bill and Susie are comfortable with their life, but they want more. Susie wants to quit her part-time job and spend more time raising her children. The $12,000 that she makes from her job barely covers the cost of childcare, but they barely make ends meet as it is. Bill has a good job processing claims at an insurance company. His life feels aimless, and he feels like there is something more. Bill sees people after a disaster, but he wants to open a small consultancy business to help other businesses prepare for and prevent major property damage. He is sure his business would succeed if he had the money to start.

Bill and Susie's financial foundation is not very strong. They live in a big house, but they wish its value would increase as fast as the cost of maintaining it. They have refinanced their 30 year mortgage a couple of times to lengthen the duration and lower the payments, but they still can't keep up with the payments.

They drive two very functional cars. By the time they pay off the loan, the cost of maintaining an older car is more than the payment, so they are constantly upgrading and acquiring more payments and more debt. They are caught in a cycle of always making a car payment. The debt payments eat up most of their monthly income.

The advantage of being comfortable with debt is you can use it for many things. Did you know you can furnish your entire home without paying a cent up front? Some of these purchases were even promised at zero interest. Bill and Susie could also use debt to acquire some of the finer things in life. They live in the desert, but they own snow skis and a motor boat. They have the finest home entertainment center with a flat screen TV, state of the art sound system, and the accompanying electronics. They have a patio that is the envy of the neighborhood with lawn furniture, the finest gas grill, and propane outdoor heaters. They have all of this leisure equipment, but they spend so much time working to pay off their toys that they can't enjoy them. Plus they constantly worry about their credit score.

Bill and Susie feel over-extended at the end of the month. If their credit cards couldn't fill the gaps, they surely wouldn't make ends meet. Their credit cards work well now, but they would work better with a slightly lower interest rate and a slightly higher credit limit. They could sell some of their stuff to avoid paying for the storage unit; but they worked hard for their things…didn't they? Bill and Susie want to pay off some of their debt and they will once Bill gets a raise at work. Oh yeah, they can hardly wait until Bill's ship comes in.

They would like to do so many things with their money. They would like to tithe ten percent to their church and give some of their money to local charities. They easily rationalize their lack of giving. "If we had any extra money, we would save for a rainy day, or for our children's education, or to retire from our dead end jobs," they say to alleviate their guilt. How could they give money away when they are this far in debt? And Bill gets frustrated every time he thinks about the small business that he lacks enough money to start.

Bill and Susie fight all the time. It's usually not over money. They stopped talking about money a long time ago. Their kids seem unhappy despite the gifts lavished upon them. They can't get ahead. They both wonder if there is more to life. "If we could just win the lottery, or if Grandma would die with $100,000 hidden in her mattress, then we could get out of this mess." But everyone knows that Bill and Susie would just find more creative ways to spend their money.

On a Rock

Steve and Jill are average people. They both work hard and earn about $50,000 per year. Steve and Jill have two kids that they love, a dog, and a cat. They own their home and have two cars. They live comfortably, but not lavishly.

Steve and Jill are comfortable with their life, but they really want more. Jill wants to quit her part-time job and spend more time raising her children. The $12,000 that she earns barely covers the cost of childcare, so it makes sense to work at home. Steve has a good job processing claims at an insurance company. Steve actually works two cubicles down from Bill. Right now Steve needs the income from his job, but he feels like there is something more. Steve sees people after a disaster, but he wants to open a small consultancy business to help other businesses prepare for and prevent major property damage. He is sure it would succeed. Bill from two cubicles down even thinks it is a good idea.

Steve and Jill have a financial foundation that is rock solid. They live in a comfortable house that fits their lifestyle. They are building equity quickly with every payment. They made a twenty percent down payment. Their mortgage is fifteen years which results in a slightly higher payment, but more of the payment is principle instead of interest and this way they build equity more quickly. They even got a better interest rate than with a thirty-year mortgage, and they will pay it off before their kids start college. They sometimes wish they had a little more room in their house, but doesn't everyone wish this?

They drive very functional cars. They always pay cash for their vehicles. Their first cars were dependable old jalopies that they slowly traded up to the cars they have now. They set aside a few dollars per month to build their auto fund for purchasing new cars and repairing the cars they drive. They appreciate the cars they drive because it is better than the old cars. Even better, they don't have any auto debt hanging over them.

Steve and Jill have never been comfortable with debt. Steve and Jill don't really worry about their credit score because they rarely use debt. Because they waited to buy their home until they had a twenty percent down payment, their income was great enough to pay cash to make it livable and then furnish it with their monthly paycheck instead of debt. Steve and Jill are secure enough to buy some of the finer things in life. Now that their kids are old enough, they saved and bought the whole family ski equipment. Steve would like to buy a boat, and he probably will when they have saved enough money. Steve and Jill spend a lot of time with their children. They don't have a fancy entertainment center or the most comfortable lawn furniture, but they devote a lot of quality time to their children. They won't always have their children around, so they invest in their children by the time they spend with them.

Steve and Jill always have more demands for their money than income, but they always make tough choices and live within their means. They never really used credit cards. Steve and Jill used a credit card for their vacations, but the company canceled the card from lack of use. Some times they long for the convenience of credit cards, especially for internet purchases, but they rarely spend impulsively because it isn't convenient. Steve and Jill would like to save more, but they aren't waiting for their ship to come in, they are actively pursuing their dreams.

They want to do so much more with their money. They currently tithe ten percent to their church, but they want to contribute to some missions at home and abroad. They give to some local charities, but there are more they would like to help. It is hard to give more, but funding their children's education and a retirement fund is also important to them. If they pay off their house, they could almost cash flow their kid's college, and really boost their retirement after their kids graduate. But Steve and Jill would rather create a job that they really love and not want to retire. They are also saving to open the small business they dream about. If they save at this rate, they are probably six months away from making it happen.

Not everything is perfect with Steve and Jill. They fight from time to time, but they always work it out. Their kids are happy, but they wish they had more things like their friends. Instead of stuff, Steve and Jill give them security, quality time, and love. They are sure there is more to life. Instead of hoping for it to happen, they are intentionally making something more happen.

The Rain, the Flood, and the Wind

Some houses built on sand become so gaudy and so grandiose that they just collapse under their own weight. Financially, they don't have the income, the planning, the controlled spending, and the savings to support the huge asset that they have built. For people like this, their financial lives can be ruined without a job loss, disability, family tragedy, market shift, or any change in circumstance. Just the weight of their overspending brings their financial house down.

Bill and Susie's house, built on sand, isn't over-extended; but it is big. They manage their mirage of wealth with some difficulty, but they have very little margin for error.

"...and the rain descended, the floods came, and the winds blew and beat on that house; and it fell. And great was its fall."

Matthew 7:27 (NKJV)

One of the hazards of living in a nation of such prosperity is that the reality of storms is difficult to find. We take note of national calamities like recessions, war, or natural disaster. But even during good times, businesses fail, people get laid off, bread winners become ill, disabled or die, and individuals suffer catastrophic property damage. Even for experts, storms are difficult to predict, but they will happen in your life.

For Bill and Susie, their storm is a job loss. The insurance company where Bill works is overstaffed and they lay off 300 people in their claims department. There is no severance and they can keep their health insurance for six months only if they pay the premium. Bill gets one more monthly paycheck of $4,000. He may draw unemployment, but that is short term and won't cover their monthly obligations and expenses.

Bill and Susie are in a bind. They can't cut back on their expenses, especially for the children, because they don't want the kids knowing anything is wrong…but the kids know. They see their parents fight all the time. It's not over money because they still don't talk about their finances. They can see this storm coming, but they still do nothing.

This layoff is devastating. With 300 other people with the same skills as Bill, there are very few job prospects. Susie's part-time job cuts back her hours and her paycheck doesn't cover their obligations. They spend their cash in about three weeks. Their credit cards are maxed out two weeks after this. They apply for a home equity line of credit, but with their missed payments, their credit score is terrible. Who would be crazy enough to loan money to someone with no income?

Bill thinks about ways to get through this crisis. He begs for relief from the bank that holds their mortgage, but they are already impatient and skeptical he will repay. He gives up on his credit cards. He doesn't look at his mail or answer his phone calls to avoid his creditors. Bill has a lot of junk he can sell. His children won't give up any of their treasures. The garage sale helps, but the proceeds are spent in less than a week. Bill becomes so desperate that he prays. After about a week with no miracle, Bill grumbles to himself, "God obviously isn't listening."

Susie is looking for different solutions. She can't take it any more. She wants a legal separation and a divorce. She tolerated the fighting when Bill supported the family, but now it isn't worth it. How did they get here? Not very long ago, they seemed to have it all; but their foundation of sand eroded quickly under the stress of the storm.

Steve and Jill's Storm

Similar to Bill and Susie, Steve and Jill can't see their storm building. The storm hits them as quickly as it hits Bill and Susie, but their circumstance is different. Their financial house is built on a rock.

Their cars are paid for, and they have no credit card debt. Their only monthly obligation is their house payment. They have six months of living expenses saved in their storehouse fund, but because they are temporarily cutting back on savings, spending, and giving, their money will probably stretch for nine months. If that doesn't last, they have some savings targeted to a new car that they could tap and extend the time to one year. They also have some long term retirement and college savings, and equity in their home that could be used; but they will not drain everything they have built.

Steve gets one more paycheck of $4,000. There is no severance and Steve won't bother with the hassle of unemployment. They can keep the company health insurance, but Steve shopped around and found cheaper health coverage. Steve has found an alternative for almost all of his benefits in anticipation of quitting his job and opening his consultancy. Jill is more torn. Her part-time income would help, but she really wants to work at home and be with her kids.

Steve and Jill are very honest with each other and with their children. They make spending cuts to stretch their money. Their kids aren't happy with most of the cuts, but they respect their parents for making the hard decisions to keep them secure. There is some tension between Steve and Jill, but they are still talking and, from a money standpoint, they will be okay.

The layoff could be devastating. With 300 other people with the same skills as Steve, there are very few job prospects. Steve and Jill aren't going to wait for their fortunes to change. They are still about $20,000 away from having enough money to open the consultancy. Steve thinks about with whom he could start his business. Bill from two cubicles down was interested in the idea, but Steve knows Bill couldn't raise any money. So Steve and Jill will make it work. They rework their business budget and cut out $15,000 in start up costs. Jill will do the administrative work to make up the other $5,000.

The business starts out slow and they tap into some of their storehouse fund to meet their obligations. After four months, Steve has all the business he can handle. Jill becomes less involved as Steve hires other assistants, and she spends more time with the kids. Steve isn't making money hand over fist, but his business grows financially and he helps dozens of others prevent property loss and damage. Steve grows his business and soon will fulfill more of his family's financial objectives.

In retrospect, Steve and Jill realize that this storm is really a blessing. Would they have had the courage to go out on their own if Steve hadn't lost his job? Their prayer is a prayer of thanksgiving; for everything good and bad that happened to them. Steve and Jill know their purpose in life and have built the financial foundation necessary to fulfill that purpose. As their financial house grows, they continually strengthen their foundation.

Building Your Financial Foundation

Your financial foundation involves several key components. A solid foundation has the following building blocks: income, choice as a consumer, charitable giving, planned spending, a storehouse fund, and savings for specific financial objectives. Your purpose is the mortar that holds your foundation together. Every part must work together. A purpose to guide your financial decisions and actions is perhaps most important to your foundation.

Financial success in this life can be difficult to quantify. Is someone who has a lot of money successful? How about someone with a lot of toys? Is someone who has measurable wealth successful? Is someone with a perception of financial security successful? The mirage of wealth that most will strive for today is very temporary with no lasting legacy in this life or beyond.

Success in life can be seen in someone who discovers their purpose and works their whole life in fulfilling that purpose. There are two types of sad and unfulfilled lives. The first type may appear successful. They have a good paying job and all the trappings of success. The more they earn, the more they spend to buy an elusive happiness. This person lacks the purpose to guide their life. They wander aimlessly; doing the things society demands of him to be successful. He never feels successful and finds very little satisfaction in his temporal life.

The second type of sad life is the person who knows his purpose, but can't view the components of their financial foundation through the prism of their purpose. They know what they want in life and may even know what money they need to start; but they can't get the financing. You hear them say things like, "If I could just catch a break…Once my ship comes in…My dreams are bigger than my money." They don't have a money problem though; they just haven't used their purpose to guide them in all parts of their financial life. If you have a plan with specific financial objectives, your purpose will dictate changes in your consumer choice, a more controlled spending plan, an increased income, a famine fund to smooth out bumps, and these tasks done to fulfill your purpose. Development of a charitable and servant's heart is a key characteristic of someone with purpose. Charitable giving, therefore, is a necessary part of developing a financial life with purpose.

These foundational aspects must be used together to fulfill your purpose. If you can't earn more, you may spend less. If you can't find money to give or save, you must revisit your spending plan and reevaluate the needs and wants in your life. You may reconsider how much you spend on your needs and cut back on some wants. These choices must be made with a focus on your purpose.

Who am I to Serve?

A key question to ask when developing your purpose is, "Who am I to serve?" How do you answer this question?

"I'm in it for myself," the jaded woman says, "I'm fed up with thinking about everyone else. From now on, I am doing everything for myself."

"Let me know how that works out for you," the financial counselor says with a sigh.

She goes out into the world looking for her share of the pie. She demands higher wages from her boss, but refuses hard work. She considers embezzlement as a way to "get hers," but decides not. She has no moralistic guide telling her of the inherent wrong, but she can't make it big from prison. She deserves much more. She has made much more money for her boss than he has paid her.

She spends impulsively. Every purchase gives her a temporary thrill, but the thrill quickly subsides and her purchase ends up in a closet or storage. When the money dries up, she turns to "free money"...credit cards and other debt. She can spend up to the limit and there are very few things the credit card companies can do to get their money back. She always has bankruptcy to fall back on.

There is really no need to save or give. Giving does nothing to increase her happiness. She used to get a thrill out of giving, but that thrill is even more temporary than impulsive buying.

As the cycle of earning, spending it all, and using debt speeds up, this woman is caught in a trap. She can't loose her credit cards, so she works harder to earn more money. With a greater income, she feels more comfortable spending. Because she has paid everything off, her credit limit is raised and she has access to more money. The cycle continues until she realizes none of this creates happiness; much less a long lasting satisfaction or fulfillment.

A similar woman, or perhaps the same woman looking for more in life, answers the question, "I will serve others."

She goes out in the world with a new attitude of servanthood. At her job, she worries less about squeezing every last penny out of her boss and serves her employer. She serves her customers everyday and these customers become very loyal to the business. Either this employer will recognize her value as an employee, or a competitor will recognize her value and entice her to his business.

She buys only what is a blessing in her life. She buys food, clothing, and shelter. She still has wants, but she only buys things that build true value in her life. Her entertainment, leisure, and travel purchases are very selective and she makes a real effort to remember unsatisfactory purchases.

With a servant's heart, giving is only natural. She tithes to her church. She has a long list of organizations that she helps with both her money and time. This is not enough, though. She is thinking of new ways to help others. It may be a business, a charity, or a ministry; she is not sure yet, but she will do more.

This is why she saves. She may save for education for skills to help people. She may save for retirement so she can go on a foreign mission when she is sixty. She may be saving to start a charity or business that serves people. Whatever it is, she is saving.

A philosopher may tell her that serving other people will satisfy a moral and ethical dimension to her life. A theologian may tell her that serving others is the only way to truly serve Christ. A businessman may tell her that creating value in other people's lives is ultimately the only way to earn money. When it is all said and done, by serving others her life has real meaning and purpose. Getting up in the morning is no longer met with dread, but with an excitement for the new adventure that the day will hold. With difficult and perplexing situations, there is a peace that passes all understanding and is a calming and stabilizing factor in her life. Her friends and family will ask what has changed in her life because they want the same kind of joy and peace.

Your Purpose and Your Money

Tying your finances to your purpose will not remove all hardship from your life. It won't necessarily make life easier, and adversity will still knock at your door...but life will be more fulfilling and productive.

Too many people work for their money. They face the drudgery of their day just to make ends meet. These people need a change of heart and a change of mind. Making your money work to fulfill your purpose gives direction and meaning to your money. Instead of green rectangles or numbers on a bank statement, your money represents your values and the things you truly value. Money spent is for a purpose. Money that is saved will be for a future goal to fulfill your purpose. Money that is given will be with the gratitude of a servant. Make your money work to fulfill your purpose in life.

The fact that you have this book in your hand says you are a person who desires to live with a purpose, to use your money to make a difference in this world, and to be a person of significance. Don't let your dreams just sit on a shelf until they become a long-lost fantasy; make the decision today to create the future you truly desire. Granted, the choices are difficult and the work is hard, but if you build your financial foundation on a solid rock, you will build prosperity not only in the realm of money, but also in every area of your life. You *can* build the financial freedom to experience your dreams, and the tools in this book will help you accomplish your goals and fulfill your purpose. And when the storms of life hit, which they invariably do, nothing will shake you because you have built your life and your financial foundation…*On a Rock*.

From the Authors

ON *THE* ROCK

If there is anything that we hoped to accomplish in this book is that a firm financial foundation involves much more than just money. Wealth is multi-pronged in its scope. We all know of people who have more money than they know what to do with, but are not wealthy in the sense of a peacefully balanced life. Finding our purpose in life really is what living is all about…the type of living that produces a balanced life. We believe that God has created you very uniquely with awesome gifts and talents. When you discover what your purpose and passions are, not only can you experience a balanced life, but also you will end up being a person of true wealth…having a solid foundation of financial security.

"On a Rock" is the title of this book, but it is also a metaphor of where our life can be positioned or what our life can be built upon. It is the belief of these authors that Jesus Christ is THE ROCK on which our life can be positioned, which will then lead to a peacefully balanced life. Our hope is that as you consider the purpose and positioning of your life, you may also consider building your life on THE ROCK.

Lynn Schaal
Gus Brackett

We would love to hear from you. Feel free contact us at:
gus@12bookbaskets.com

APPENDIX

From Chapter 4: Tithing

Tithe = before tax income × .10

A simpler means of determining the amount to tithe is to figure your before tax income and move the decimal one place to the left.

> Ex. If your before tax monthly income is $2250. Your monthly tithe would be:
> Tithe = $2250 × .10
> = $225

From Chapter 5: Spending Plan

Steps for creating a spending plan:

Step one: Create an income statement
Step two: Estimate your current expenses
Step three: Prioritize your outflow categories
Step four: Allocate a dollar amount for each category

From Chapter 7: From Purpose to Action

Step one: Determine your purpose
Step two: Set goals
Step three: Analyze your goals
Step four: Define your objectives
Step five: Action

From Chapter 8: Saving

Storehouse Fund = (Monthly Income – monthly taxes, savings, and giving) × number of months

Ex. Your monthly income is $2000. Taxes are $400, tithe is $200, and savings are $400. This person wants five months living expense:

Storehouse Fund =

($2000 – ($400 + $200 + $400)) × 5 months.
= $1000 × 5 months
= $5000 storehouse fund

Five Factors for Creating a Savings Plan:

1. Estimate your current savings
2. Place a dollar amount on your objective
3. Establish a time frame
4. Prioritize your savings
5. Determine your monthly contribution

Monthly contribution =

total needed ÷ the years until needed ÷ 12
Ex. The saving objective requires $12,000. The money is needed in 2 years.

Monthly contribution = $12,000 ÷ 2 ÷ 12
= $500 per month

Inflation adjusted Monthly Contribution

Monthly contribution =

Total needed × inflation factor ÷ the years until needed ÷ 12

Ex. The savings objective requires $40,000. The money is needed in 20 years.

Monthly contribution =

= $40,000 × 2.19 ÷ 20 years ÷ 12

Note: The inflation factor table is on page 146.

= $365

Using a financial calculator is more precise. If you don't know how to use one, use the inflation factor for a ballpark figure to get started saving.